NO EASY DAY

The Best and Most Comprehensive Book on Military Recruiting Ever Written, by a Marine Who Has Actually Done it.

Jacob G. McClinton

ISBN: 9798853948464

DEDICATION

With a heavy heart and deepest love, I dedicate this book to my beloved mother, Toni McClinton. During my years on recruiting duty, just a few minutes from my hometown, I spent little time with my family, and you in particular. Tragically, during my final months on recruiting duty, you were murdered. I will always regret not having made more time for you and my family during those years, and I dedicate this book to your memory. Rest in peace, Mom. I love you always.

CONTENTS

ACKNOWLEDGMENTS

I author this book to help the men and women who have served or will serve, as 8411s in the Marine Corps. This book, a culmination of six years of research and reflection, is my humble attempt to impart wisdom and practical tools to make their journey on recruiting duty a little easier.

Firstly, to my wife Krystle, I cannot express enough how much your love, support and sacrifice has meant to me. You have made our home a sanctuary and taken care of our family while I have been away, whether it be in the deserts of the Middle East or on the streets of our nation. Thank you for all that you do.

To Thomas McKenzie, my leader and mentor, I am eternally grateful for your honesty, guidance, and mentorship. Your sage advice and unwavering support have been invaluable to me, and I would not be where I am today without you.

To my brothers and sisters in RSS Santa Rosa, RSS Fairfield, RSS American Canyon, and RSS Metro East I am honored to have served alongside each and every one of you. Despite any differences we may have had, we accomplished the mission together. Thank you for your tireless efforts and dedication, and for putting up with me.

And finally, to the 8411's currently on the streets today, grinding through an unforgiving job, I want to extend my deepest gratitude and respect. I know that the work you do is not easy, and that the sacrifices you make are great. You are valuable members of the team.

1 INTRODUCTION

Welcome to the world of Marine Corps Recruiting! If you're reading this book, you're likely a Canvassing Recruiter who has been thrown into the deep end with nothing more than a MCEOB, some benefit tags, and a somewhat shaky understanding of MC3. But don't worry, I understand that recruiting duty is hard, and I'm here to help make it a little easier for you.

I know that recruiting duty can be a roller coaster of emotions. There may be months when you feel like you're on top of the world, writing contracts left and right and making mission with ease. But then there are those rough months where it feels like everything is against you and you cannot catch a break. Some days it feels like it will never end, and you wonder if you will ever make it through to the other side.

But every tour on recruiting duty ends eventually, and when it does, you'll be able to look back on all that you accomplished and be proud of the hard work you put in. Even on those tough days, when it feels like you're never going to write a contract or make mission, remember that it's all temporary. Keep pushing forward, stay positive, and eventually, you'll see the light at the end of the tunnel.

If you follow the tips and strategies that I'll be sharing with you in this book, your time on recruiting duty will be much less painful. And remember, the true mark of a successful tour on recruiting duty is not just about making mission and rolling bones. It's about having your career and your family still intact when it's all said and done.

So don't give up! With the right mindset and tools, you can not only survive your tour on recruiting duty, but thrive. And when you get that fancy red and blue ribbon, you'll be able to look back with pride on the hard work you put in and the people you helped bring into the Corps.

This book is structured by providing anecdotes on a topic and then reflecting upon that anecdote with specific strategies you can use to make yourself more effective on the streets. I made the sections short; this is so you and your team can cover a chapter in a single RSS Training. Some of these anecdotes are my own experiences from the duty, some are experiences I have been told by other recruiters, some are from points in history long ago, and some are complete fiction, but all of them are crafted specifically to make you, the reader of this book, better at recruiting for the Marine Corps in the Digital Age. This book is the culmination of two recruiting tours, and more than five years of study, rewrites, edits, and research, I hope you find it valuable. Good luck, and let's get started!

2 LEVERAGING TECHNOLOGY

Chapter Introduction

Marine Corps Recruiting must embrace technology if it hopes to remain relevant in the coming years. The world is constantly changing and evolving, and the military is no exception. The use of technology in recruiting has become increasingly important and this trend is only expected to continue in the future.

One of the key factors that have made it necessary for Marine Corps Recruiting to embrace technology is the increased competition it has faced in the recruiting environment. In the past, the military was often a top choice for young people looking to serve their country and gain valuable skills and experience after graduating high school. However, in recent years, other industries and sectors have started offering similar benefits, making it harder for the military to attract top talent and meet its recruiting goals. To stay competitive and continue to attract top talent, Marine Corps Recruiting must embrace technology and use it to reach a wider audience and better engage with potential recruits.

The use of technology can help Marine Corps Recruiting to overcome these challenges and remain competitive in the recruiting environment. By leveraging technology, the Marine Corps can reach a wider audience and better engage with potential recruits. This can include using social media to connect with young people, using online forms to capture prospect data, and using mapping software to identify trends and patterns of recruits.

Another reason why it is imperative for the Marine Corps to embrace technology is that the new era of recruits are digital natives who spend a significant amount of time online. According to a study by Common Sense Media, high school students in the United States spend an average of nearly nine hours a day using electronic media, including social media, streaming video, and online gaming. This means that most of their time is spent on digital devices, and they are likely to be more receptive to recruitment efforts that are delivered through these channels. By embracing technology and using it to reach out to potential recruits, the Marine Corps can better engage with this digitally savvy audience and stay competitive in the recruiting environment.

Over the course of the following few chapters, we will delve into the specific ways in which technology can be used to improve recruiting efforts for you, the canvassing recruiter on the ground. These tips and strategies have been developed through my own experiences as a recruiter over the course of 36 months on recruiting duty from 2017 to 2021 and now on my second tour which I started in early 2023. We will cover a range of topics, including the use of social media to connect with potential recruits, the benefits of using online recruiting tools and data analytics, and strategies for adapting to changing demographics and the evolving needs of potential recruits. By following these recommendations and leveraging technology in an effective and strategic manner, you can better engage with potential recruits, streamline the recruitment process, and stay competitive in a constantly changing environment.

Instagram

Anecdote – It Worked for Me

When I first hit the streets in January 2018, I was always looking for easier ways to reach prospects, and I found Instagram. As a result of using Instagram, I was named the Rookie Recruiter of the Year for Recruiting Station San Francisco after writing 36 contracts in just 9 months. This was a huge accomplishment for me, and I know that a big part of my success was due to my use of the platform.

When I first started using Instagram as a recruitment tool, I tried a variety of different techniques to see what would work best. One of the first things I did was pay for Instagram Ads. While these ads did reach a wide audience, I found that they didn't generate much interest or engagement from potential recruits. I also tried collaborating with other recruiters on Instagram, but that didn't seem to have much of an impact either because the followers I got from collaborating with them were in the other recruiter's AO, not my own.

One of the biggest wastes of time I found was spending hours following random students and hoping they would follow me back. This rarely worked, and even when it did, it rarely led to any meaningful engagement or interest in the Marine Corps. Looking back now I cannot think of a more useless way to spend your time on recruiting duty than the so-called "follow/unfollow" method. Similarly, going live on Instagram all the time randomly didn't seem to have much of an impact. If there was a trophy for trying things on Instagram that didn't work, I probably would have won it.

Despite these setbacks, I was eventually able to find a few strategies that really worked for me. One of the most effective strategies was growing my Instagram page locally. Instead of trying to gain as many followers as I could, I focused on attracting followers only from my local area. This meant no more using big hashtags like #usmc or #marines or trying to "blow up" on Instagram. Instead, I used hashtags that were specific to the city I worked in, such as the physical location I was at, #sanfranciscobayarea, or the names of high schools I worked in, #tamalpaishighschool. This allowed me to connect with people near me instead of people far away like some motivated 12-year-old kid in Fort Worth, Texas.

Another effective strategy was advertising my social media handles during class talks and table displays. Whenever I had the opportunity to speak to students or set up a booth at a career fair, I made sure to display my Instagram page and let them know where they could follow me to learn more about the Marine Corps. I didn't beg for followers, but I made it easy for people to find me and follow me if they were interested.

Another key to my success on Instagram was staying on brand. When I posted content on a regular basis about the Marine Corps, rather than focusing on myself, I found that more and more applicants were reaching out to me. I learned that potential recruits were more interested in hearing about what the Marine Corps had to offer, rather than just seeing pictures of me, and my kids, or my personal life.

Finally, producing valuable and well-thought-out content was crucial to my success on Instagram. Using a good microphone, good lighting, and presenting ideas or solutions that were controversial or thought-provoking, generated the best results. One video that I can confirm generated at least three contracts for me by itself, possibly more, was when I broke down how someone could get their bachelor's degree faster by enlisting in the Marine Corps than they could at a four-year university. I spent some time and produced a video this video was well-researched and presented in a clear and concise manner. It really resonated with prospects and poolees who were looking for alternative paths to getting their degree.

In addition to these strategies, I also found it helpful to engage with my followers on a regular basis. This meant responding to comments and messages, as well as liking and commenting on other people's posts. This helped to build a sense of community on my Instagram page, and it also helped to establish me as a trusted and reliable source of information about the Marine Corps.

Despite the challenges, I was able to achieve significant success thanks to my use of Instagram. By focusing on attracting followers in my local community, staying "on brand", and producing valuable content, I was able to effectively reach and engage with potential recruits. While it took some trial and error to find what worked best for me, the effort was worth it, as it allowed me to connect with many qualified prospects and help them achieve their goals of serving their country.

Reflection

Now that you heard what I did when I was on the duty, how can you use this tool to your advantage? I have had a few years off the streets at this point and a lot of time to reflect. I believe you can do a lot of things much better than I ever could. Here are some specific ways that Marine Corps Recruiters can use and refine the strategies I mentioned above to recruit more people:

1. Use local hashtags: Use hashtags related to your city, your schools, and things specific to the community you serve in your posts and stories. This will help you reach people who are interested in these topics and may be interested in joining the Marine Corps.

2. Collaborate with local businesses and influencers: Post content with local businesses and influencers who align with the values and mission of the Marine Corps. This can help you reach a larger and more targeted audience of potential recruits.

3. Engage with your local community: Follow and interact with other local accounts and participate in local events and activities. This can help you build relationships and get noticed by more people in your area who may be interested in joining the Marine Corps.

4. Use Instagram's location feature: Use the location feature to tag your posts and stories with the location of your recruiting station or events. This will help people in your area discover your content more easily and learn more about the opportunities available in the Marine Corps.

5. Advertise where you will be: Post the time events you are hosting in your local community and encourage potential recruits to show up in person. Events could include pool functions, physical fitness events, or other activities that showcase the values and opportunities of the organization.

6. Post high-quality, engaging content: Consistently post high-quality, engaging content that showcases the values, goals, and opportunities of the Marine Corps. Share stories and photos that highlight the camaraderie, discipline, and leadership skills that are developed in the organization.

You may have read through that list and thought, "well, what exactly do I post?", so here are some ideas of types of content to post on Instagram that I believe the following in your community may see as valuable:

1. Highlight the core values of the Marine Corps: The Marine Corps has a strong set of core values, including honor, courage, and

commitment. Share posts that highlight these values and show how they guide the actions and decisions of Marines. You can also share quotes or stories that demonstrate the importance of these values in the Marine Corps.

2. Show off the rigorous training that Marines undergo: Potential recruits often have a strong desire to push themselves physically and mentally, and the training that Marines undergo can be a major draw. Share photos and videos of Marines participating in training exercises, such as the Crucible or Marine Corps Recruit Depot (MCRD) Parris Island.

3. Share stories from current and former Marines: Personal stories from Marines who have served can be very powerful in attracting potential recruits. Specifically, Marines who are living in your community. You will be surprised how many people in your community served in the past. LinkedIn is a great source for this. If you search people based on city and then filter it by "companies previously worked at" you will have a list of professionals in your city who served in the Corps in the past. Reach out to them and ask for an interview about their experiences in the Corps and how it has shaped their lives.

4. Highlight the opportunities for education and career advancement: Many potential recruits are looking for ways to advance their education and careers, and the Marine Corps offers numerous opportunities in these areas. Share posts that highlight the education and career advancement opportunities available to Marines, such as the Post-9/11 GI Bill, tuition assistance, and USMAP.

5. Share tips and advice for those considering joining the Marine Corps: Since you have been through recruit training yourself, you likely have valuable insights and advice to share with potential recruits. Create posts that offer tips and advice for those considering joining the Marine Corps, such as how to prepare for the physical fitness test or how to prepare yourself mentally for recruit training.

6. Offer behind-the-scenes looks at the daily life of a Marine: Many potential recruits are curious about what it's really like to be a Marine on a day-to-day basis. Share posts that offer a behind-the-scenes look at the daily life of a Marine, such as what they eat, where they live, and what they do when they're not training.

7. Share information about the various roles and career paths available in the Marine Corps: The Marine Corps offers a wide range of career paths, from combat to logistics to intelligence. Each MOS could be its own piece of content. Share posts that highlight the various roles and career paths available in the Marine Corps and how Marines can progress through the ranks.

8. Share success stories from Marines who have excelled in their careers: Seeing examples of successful Marines can be a powerful motivator for potential recruits. Bonus points if those people are in your local community. Share posts that feature success stories from Marines who have excelled in their careers, whether it's through promotions, awards, or other achievements.

9. Highlight the camaraderie and sense of community in the Marine Corps: Many potential recruits are looking for a sense of

belonging and purpose, and the Marine Corps provides both. Share posts that showcase the strong camaraderie and sense of community within the Corps, such as photos of Marines working together or participating in team-building activities.

In addition to these ideas, it's also important to remember to keep your content authentic and engaging. Steer away from "low-brow" content such as dancing, comedy, or other "cringe" posts. It may get some viewership, but it does not translate well to our brand, a professional warfighting organization. Show potential recruits what it's really like to be a Marine, and be transparent about the challenges and sacrifices that come with serving in the Corps. By sharing real and meaningful content, you can build trust and authenticity with potential recruits and create a strong connection with them.

Don't forget to engage with your followers. By engaging with your followers and responding to comments and questions, you can create a sense of community and show that you're approachable and willing to help.

Instagram can be a powerful tool for attracting potential recruits to the Marine Corps. By sharing a mix of personal stories about the Marine Corps, training and career information, and behind-the-scenes looks at the daily life of a Marine, you can showcase the values, opportunities, and experiences that make the Corps unique and appealing. By being authentic and engaging, you can build trust and create a strong connection with potential recruits, ultimately helping you make mission.

Mapping Software

Anecdote – Operation Inherent Resolve, First Trip

I remember the first time I was exposed to mapping software's power like yesterday. I was a young sergeant with no experience in the Middle East, having spent my first enlistment stationed in Japan. I was suddenly told that I needed to get on a plane to deploy in support of Operation Inherent Resolve, filling in for someone else who couldn't go. At the time, I didn't really know much about the operation or what to expect. All I knew was that I was excited and needed to pack my bags and get on a plane as soon as possible. It was a bit of a shock to the system, but I was ready for the challenge.

Two weeks later, I found myself getting off a plane in the middle of the night in some far-off desert, feeling the heat of the night air on my skin. I had never been to the Middle East before, and the monotony of it all was surprising. Arriving there was like stepping into an old grocery store that was about to close, none of the contractors seemed happy to be there and all the equipment looked like it was out of date and had been used one too many times.

After getting some sleep in my bunk, I was brought in for and in brief with my Officer-In-Charge. I was a member of the intelligence section of the Special Purpose Marine Air Ground Task Force – Crisis Response Central Command. My job was to collect and disseminate Human Intelligence and Counterintelligence information in Iraq and Syria. I was assigned to work with a team of analysts, and

I quickly got to know them and learn the ropes.

One of the things that really stood out to me was how the analysts were able to use mapping software to visualize data coming in from intelligence collectors. They took numbers on a spreadsheet and turned them into maps that were worth reading. What would have taken an hour for the commander to understand on paper was understood in just ten seconds on the map software. Across the entire Combined Joint Operating Area - which covered most of Iraq - the commander could see the locations of ISIS weapon caches, hideouts, potential targets, and friendly forces. Everything he needed to decide was right in front of him, all thanks to the power of mapping software.

I was amazed by how effective it was. The commander could see exactly what was going on across the whole area of operations, and it made it much easier for him to make informed decisions. It was clear to me that this kind of technology was incredibly valuable in a battlefield setting. As the weeks went by, I got more and more involved in the intelligence gathering and analysis process. I was a collector and not an analyst, so I never needed to use the software myself. In my free time though, I learned how to use it, and I was able to contribute to the team in a meaningful way. It was a challenging and rewarding experience, and I felt like I was really making a difference.

This was just one example of how the mapping software helped us to effectively target and eliminate ISIS militants in Iraq. It was an invaluable tool, and I'm grateful for the opportunity to have been a part of the team that used it to make a difference.

Eventually, my deployment came to an end, and it was time for me to head back home. After my deployment in support of Operation Inherent Resolve, I was ordered to recruiting duty. It was a new challenge that I was eager to tackle. I knew this kind of technology could be incredibly valuable in a recruiting setting, so I made it my mission to find ways to use it to help me in my role. I quickly realized that mapping software could be a powerful tool for identifying areas with a high potential for recruitment and identifying patterns and trends that could help me target my efforts more effectively.

Reflection

Those assets and enlistment maps hanging in the SNCOIC office, what decisions are they influencing? How are you using them to target your recruiting efforts? If they answer to those questions are "none" and "you're not using them" then I think it is time for a change. I think you should convert them to digital Assets and Enlistment Maps. In my experience, Assets and Enlistment Maps are not being used as effectively as they could be, or even at all. Mapping software has come a long way in recent years, and it is now possible to create dynamic, interactive maps that can be accessed and updated in real-time. This can be much more useful than a static map with pins, which can quickly become outdated and may not provide the level of detail and context that is needed to make informed decisions.

Presently, Assets and Enlistment Maps are just pieces of foamboard with pins, it may be worth considering updating them to a more modern, digital format. This could involve using mapping software like Google Earth to create an interactive map that can be accessed by all relevant parties, and that can be updated as needed. This would likely require some initial investment in terms of time and resources, but the benefits could be significant in terms of increased efficiency and effectiveness.

In any case, it's important to remember that the Assets and Enlistment Maps are just one tool among many, and they should be used in a way that makes sense for your office and its needs. If they are not providing the level of value that you need, or if you are only putting the pins in to pass a Systematic Recruiting Inspection, it may be worth considering alternative approaches or technologies that can better support your mission.

There are several ways that Marine Corps Recruiters could benefit from transitioning from a static map with pins to mapping software like Google Earth and plotting the addresses of students:

1. Increased accuracy and timeliness: With a dynamic, digital map, recruiters can access real-time data and updates, rather than relying on a static map that may not reflect the most current information. This can help to ensure that recruiters have access to the most accurate and up-to-date data available.

2. Targeting recruiting efforts: By visualizing the locations of students on a map, recruiters can identify areas with a high

concentration of potential recruits and target their efforts accordingly. This can help to ensure that recruiters are maximizing their time and resources.

3. Better visualization and analysis: Mapping software like Google Earth allows for the visualization of data in a way that is more intuitive and easier to understand. Recruiters can use the software to identify patterns and trends in enlistment data and to target their efforts more effectively.

4. Increased efficiency: With a digital map, recruiters can access and update information more quickly and easily, without having to manually update a physical map. This can save time and improve efficiency.

5. Improved outreach efforts: By understanding the locations of students, recruiters can better plan outreach efforts, such as conducting home visits or sending out direct mail. More on this can be found in Chapter 4 of this book. This can help to ensure that they are reaching as many potential recruits as possible.

6. Improved collaboration: Digital maps can be shared and accessed by multiple users, allowing recruiters to collaborate and share information more effectively.

Transitioning to mapping software like Google Earth and plotting the addresses of students could provide several benefits for Marine Corps Recruiters, including increased accuracy, better visualization and analysis, increased efficiency, improved outreach efforts, and improved collaboration. It is worth considering whether this kind of technology could help the Marine Corps to make mission more effectively.

Linkedin, Undervalued and Underused

Anecdote – Non-Profit Sales Work

I have a friend who had the opportunity to work with a non-profit organization that helps transitioning service members find employment as they exit the military. His primary responsibility was to reach out to executive-level leadership at various companies and try to secure appointments for his team to speak with them about partnering with the non-profit.

At first, he was a little intimidated by this task. He had never worked in a non-profit before and wasn't sure if he had the necessary skills to reach out to these high-level executives. However, as he started to work with his boss and the rest of the team, he quickly saw the power of LinkedIn in helping them achieve their goals.

One of the first things he learned was the importance of building his own personal brand on LinkedIn. According to a survey by LinkedIn, 84% of professionals believe that building a personal brand is important for their career. He made sure to update his profile with his current job and any relevant experience or skills that he had. He also started connecting with other professionals in his field and joining relevant LinkedIn groups. This helped him establish himself as a credible and trustworthy source of information, which was crucial when it came time to reach out to executives and ask for their time.

Once he had established his personal brand on LinkedIn, he began using the platform to connect with executives at various companies. According to LinkedIn, 85% of professionals say that they are open to hearing opportunities. This made it relatively easy for him to reach out to executives and explain why he was contacting them. Most of the time, they were more than happy to speak with him and schedule a time for his boss to speak.

One of the things that really impressed him about LinkedIn was how effective it was at helping his team reach the right people. By targeting their outreach to specific industries and job titles, they were able to make sure that they were speaking with the decision-makers who had the power to make a difference for their organization. According to a survey by LinkedIn, 59% of professionals say that LinkedIn is their top choice for finding new business opportunities. This was the case for my friend and his non-profit, as LinkedIn proved to be an invaluable tool in helping his team connect with the right people and secure important partnerships.

As he continued to work with the non-profit and I was able to see the power of LinkedIn in helping him reach the right people and making a difference, I thought about how this same concept could be applied to Marine Corps recruiting. Marine Corps recruiters are always looking for ways to connect with teachers and staff at local high schools as well as parents in the local community, LinkedIn could be an excellent platform for them to connect with these influencers and showcase the benefits of serving in the Marine Corps. By building a strong personal brand and using LinkedIn to target their outreach to specific industries and job titles, recruiters could effectively reach the right people and partner with them to help find prospects.

Reflection

As a Marine Corps recruiter, it's important to use every available resource to reach potential recruits and make a lasting impression. While it may seem that LinkedIn is not a valuable tool in your recruiting efforts due to its low usage among Generation Z, the platform presents a unique opportunity to connect with the influencers in a prospect's life.

According to a survey conducted by the Pew Research Center, only about 20% of young adults aged 18 to 29 use LinkedIn, compared to about 50% of adults aged 30 and older. This may lead recruiters to believe that the platform is not worth their time and effort. However, this assumption is short-sighted and ignores the fact that LinkedIn is a powerful tool for connecting with parents, teachers, school staff, members of the school board, and other influencers who play a vital role in a prospect's decision-making process.

Imagine being able to connect with a high school teacher or guidance counselor who could recommend a student join the Marine Corps. By building a relationship with these influencers on LinkedIn, you can not only increase the visibility of the Marine Corps within their network but also gain valuable insights and recommendations for potential recruits. These influencers are likely to be more active on LinkedIn and may be more receptive to communication from recruiters on the platform. In addition, by targeting influencers rather than the recruits themselves, you can reach a wider audience and potentially expand your pool of qualified prospects.

But how can you effectively utilize LinkedIn as a recruiter? Here are a few tips to get you started:

1. Create a professional LinkedIn profile with a recent and appropriate photo and highlight your background and accomplishments as a Marine. This will help to establish your credibility and attract potential connections.

2. Connect with influencers in the schools and communities you are targeting for recruitment, such as teachers, guidance counselors, school board members, and community leaders. Personalize your message and explain how the connection could be mutually beneficial.

3. Engage with your network regularly by commenting on their posts and sharing your own content and updates about the Marine Corps. This helps to establish relationships and increase visibility.

4. Share information about the Marine Corps, including job opportunities, training programs, and events, on LinkedIn to attract potential recruits and address their questions or concerns.

5. Join relevant LinkedIn groups and actively participate in

discussions to increase your visibility and establish yourself as a thought leader.

6. Use LinkedIn's advanced search features to target specific groups of people based on location, job title, industry, and other factors, to identify and connect with influencers in specific schools or cities.

Overall, while it may seem that LinkedIn is not a valuable tool for Marine Corps recruiters due to low usage among Generation Z, the platform presents a unique opportunity to connect with the influencers in a recruit's life. By establishing a strong presence on LinkedIn, connecting with influencers, and regularly engaging with your network, you can effectively utilize the platform to increase the visibility of the Marine Corps and attract more prospects. Don't overlook this valuable resource in your recruiting efforts.

Using YouTube for the DEP

Anecdote – The Inspiration for YouTube Content

This chapter is about using YouTube to build a stronger Pool Program, but to tell you that first I need to talk about where my philosophy for a good Pool Program came from. When I was on "the streets", I often heard career recruiters flapping their gums about their strategies for taking care of the Pool. To be honest, I didn't think much of it at the time. I had a love-hate relationship with the career recruiters. Most of them just said, "do more, better", which I believe is useless advice. On one hand, I respected their experience and dedication to the job. On the other hand, I often found them to be insincere and full of empty promises. Many of them acted like they had all the answers, but when it came time to put their words into action, they seemed to disappear. Most of them seemed as if they wanted to stay as far away from a mission letter as possible.

That's why I was so grateful to have a few 8412s who broke that mold. Mentors like Jeremy Shorten, Thomas McKenzie, and Carb. These three career recruiters were different from most of their colleagues. They cared about the recruiters on a mission letter and were always willing to share their knowledge and experience. They often took the time to sit down with me and offer guidance and support, helping me to become a better leader and build a stronger pool program.

One of the things that set Jeremy, Thomas, and Carb apart from the rest was their focus on building relationships with their poolees. In addition to building relationships, Jeremy, Thomas, and John also stressed the importance of structure and discipline within the pool program. They taught me to ensure that my poolees knew exactly when and where to be and to hold them accountable for their actions. They stressed the importance of making weekly contact, whether in person or through phone calls or email, to keep my poolees motivated and engaged.

But perhaps the most valuable lesson I learned from Jeremy, Thomas, and Carb was the importance of leading my poolees like Marines. Thomas often told me, "They're not idiots. If you want them to act like little kids, treat them like little kids. If you want them to act like Marines, treat them like Marines." This simple but powerful piece of advice stuck with me, and I made a conscious effort to hold my poolees to high standards and expect the best from them.

I took the lessons and guidance from Jeremy, Thomas, and Carb to heart and worked hard to implement their strategies in my own pool program. And I have to say, the results were truly impressive. My poolees were more engaged and motivated than ever before, and I saw a significant increase in the number of Poolees joining my pool program. I will speak more about their specific advice and techniques for building a good Pool Program in a later chapter of this book.

However, looking back, I realize that I missed out on a lot of contracts by not combining their advice of the Pool Program with the power of video content. With so much of the younger generation spending their time online, YouTube was a critical platform for conveying messages to poolees. If I had embraced the importance of video content from the beginning, I have no doubt that my recruiting efforts would have been more successful.

In the end, I learned that the adage "do more, better" was not enough. It was important to think creatively and use all the tools at my disposal to reach potential recruits. I am grateful to have had mentors like Jeremy, Thomas, and Carb, their guidance and support were instrumental in my success as a recruiter, and I am forever grateful for the lessons they taught me.

Reflection

One of the ways that Marine Corps Recruiters can use YouTube to enhance the DEP is by creating and sharing videos that provide information about the program and what it entails. These videos can help individuals who have already enlisted understand what they can expect while enrolled in the DEP and how it can help them prepare for their future service.

Some ideas for YouTube videos that Marine Corps Recruiters could create to enhance the DEP include:

1. Overview of the DEP: A video that provides an overview of the DEP, including what it is, how it works, and what individuals can expect while enrolled in the program. This could include information about the physical and mental preparation requirements, as well as the standards of conduct and appearance that DEP participants are expected to adhere to. A big thing to note is the MANDATORY attendance of Monthly Pool Functions and Weekly PT Sessions.

2. Physical training requirements: A video that explains the physical training requirements for the DEP such as when and where they need to be for Weekly Physical Training and how individuals can prepare for them. This could include tips for training at home or in a gym, as well as information about the PFT and CFT that individuals will need to pass before shipping off to recruit training.

3. Mental preparation: A video that focuses on the mental preparation required for the DEP and boot camp. This could include information about books they are mandated to read while in the DEP

and the mental toughness that individuals will need to make it through recruit training, as well as tips for staying motivated and focused during the DEP. Recruit training can be physically and mentally demanding, and it is important for individuals to be mentally prepared for the challenges they will face. This may include developing strong problem-solving skills, learning to work effectively as part of a team, and learning to adapt to new and unfamiliar situations.

4. Frequently asked questions: A video that answers common questions about the DEP, such as what happens if an individual is unable to meet the physical or mental preparation requirements, or how to select a job. Be completely transparent about the way the Marine Corps assigns jobs. It can be helpful for DEP participants to have access to accurate and up-to-date information about the program, and a video that addresses common questions and concerns can be a valuable resource.

5. Success stories from DEP participants. These could be short videos or vignettes featuring individuals who have successfully completed the DEP and gone on to excel in boot camp and beyond. These stories can be inspiring and motivating for others who are considering joining the DEP and can help to illustrate the benefits and rewards of the program.

By creating and sharing a range of informative and inspiring videos, recruiters can provide DEP participants with the information and resources they need to succeed in their military careers.

Some people will say just show your Poolees other videos on YouTube, but there are several potential benefits to making videos about the DEP yourself, rather than simply showing Poolees other videos.

First, by creating your own videos, you can tailor the content to the specific needs and interests of your Poolees. You can ensure that the information you provide is relevant, accurate, and up-to-date, and can focus on topics that are most likely to be of interest to Poolees. This can be especially valuable if you are working with a diverse group of individuals who may have different needs and goals.

Second, by creating your own videos, you could showcase your own experiences and expertise as a recruiter. This can help to build trust and credibility with Poolees and can help to establish you as a valuable resource for information and support.

Third, by creating your own videos, you can create a cohesive and consistent message about your DEP and what it entails. Every DEP is a little different and this can help to ensure that Poolees have a clear understanding of the program and what is expected of them and can help to prevent confusion or misunderstandings.

Finally, by creating your own videos, you can use the videos as part of a larger marketing and recruitment strategy. You can use the videos to show parents and teachers and to showcase the benefits of the DEP and the Marine Corps in general. You can also use the videos to promote your own recruiting efforts and to connect with potential Poolees. Creating your own videos about the DEP can be a powerful way to engage with Poolees and support their preparation for military service, but what if you have no video editing experience?

I thought you may be wondering that so here are five tips on making high-quality YouTube videos:

1. Start with a clear idea or concept: Before you start filming, it's important to have a clear idea of what you want your video to be about and what message you want to convey. This will help you stay focused and ensure that your video is coherent and well-organized.

2. Invest in good equipment: High-quality audio and video are essential for a successful YouTube video. Invest in a good camera, microphone, and lighting equipment to ensure that your video looks and sounds professional. Good lighting is particularly important, as it can help to set the mood and atmosphere of your video and can also help to make your subject look more attractive and natural. High-quality audio is also essential, as poor audio quality can be very distracting and can make it difficult for viewers to understand what is being said.

3. Practice good lighting and composition: Pay attention to the lighting and composition of your shots to make sure that your video looks visually appealing. Use natural light whenever possible and use a tripod to keep your camera steady. Experiment with different lighting setups and angles to find the best look for your video.

4. Edit your video carefully: Editing is an important part of the video-making process, and it can make a big difference in the quality of your final product. Use video editing software to cut out any

unnecessary footage, add transitions, and polish your video to make it look professional.

5. Use captions and annotations: Captions and annotations can help to make your video more accessible to a wider audience and can also help to keep viewers engaged. Use these features to highlight key points or to provide additional information about your video.

A good resource for how to make engaging content for social media is the Communication Strategy (ComStrat) Marine Organic to your Recruiting Station. There are several reasons why Marine Corps recruiters should enlist the help of their ComStrat team when making YouTube videos.

The ComStrat team is specifically trained and equipped to handle the unique challenges and opportunities of modern communications, including social media and video production. This means that they have the skills and expertise needed to create high-quality, effective videos that will engage and inform potential recruits. By enlisting the help of the ComStrat team, recruiters can ensure that their videos are professional and effective at conveying their message.

The ComStrat team is well-versed in the latest trends and best practices in social media and video production, which means that they can help recruiters to create videos that are relevant and engaging to their target audience. This can be especially important when it comes to recruiting younger individuals who are more likely to use social media and YouTube as their primary sources of information.

The ComStrat team is able to provide recruiters with a range of resources and support, including access to equipment and software, as well as training and guidance on how to use these tools effectively. This can help recruiters to create high-quality videos that are on par with those produced by professional marketing and media companies, which can help to increase the impact and reach of their videos. Enlisting the help of the ComStrat team can be a valuable asset for Marine Corps recruiters looking to create high-quality YouTube videos that are effective at attracting and informing potential recruits.

Google Maps

Anecdote One – Army Got the Upper Hand

A brand-new Marine Corps recruiter had just checked into his RSS and was determined to reach as many potential recruits as possible. After a week went by, he uncovered something that made him furious. He discovered that the phone number for his PCS had been changed on both Apple and Google maps to the Army recruiter's office next door. He had no idea who was responsible for changing the number, but it was clear that someone in the Army office was trying to poach from the Marine Corps to their own office. He got angry. He could only imagine how many potential contracts were lost due to this misdirection, and he knew of no way to determine how long it had been going on. He thought even one was too many and was determined to fix the problem as soon as possible.

He contacted both Apple and Google to have the number changed to his government cell phone, and then he marched next door to the Army office to confront the issue head-on. As he entered the office, he was greeted by a Sergeant First Class who oversaw the operation. He explained the situation to him and expressed his frustration at the mix-up. To his surprise, he seemed genuinely surprised by the issue and assured the Marine Corps Recruiter that he had no idea what had happened.

Despite his anger, he decided to try and handle the situation at the lowest levels and not escalate it any further. He agreed to not elevate the issue and let it go but made it clear that he expected better from the Army in the future. The Sergeant First Class apologized for the mistake and assured him that it would not happen again. He left the office feeling a bit better, but he couldn't shake the feeling that he had lost out on many potential recruits due to this mix-up. As he returned to his office, he made a mental note to double-check all his contact information and to keep a closer eye on any potential issues that might arise.

Anecdote Two – A Victimless Crime

After performing well as a canvassing recruiter, a recruiter was selected to become a SNCOIC. It was a great opportunity, and they were excited to step into the new role. However, as they prepared to leave their PCS and take on their new office, they made a decision that they would soon regret deeply. Nobody was backfilling them as a recruiter in their office, and the PCS they were working out of would be empty for the foreseeable future. In a moment of selfishness, they changed the number for their old office on Google and Apple maps to one of their new recruiters, even though that office was not theirs anymore.

In effect, they were trying to steal contracts from their old team to help their new team - or rather, to help themselves. Unfortunately, their actions were eventually discovered by the RSS they had left behind. After about two weeks, the Assistant Recruiter Instructor, confronted them about it.

As he approached them, they could see the anger and disappointment in his eyes. They knew that they had let the ARI down, and they were filled with shame and remorse.

"What were you thinking?" he demanded. "How could you do something like this? Do you have any idea how much damage you've caused to your team and your reputation?" They were ashamed. "I'm sorry, Top," they said. "I don't know what came over me. I was just trying to help his new team, but I realize now that it was a selfish and dishonest thing to do."

The ARI sighed and shook his head. "I don't know if I can trust you anymore," he said. "You need to make this right. You need to make amends for your actions and do everything in your power to rebuild your broken trust. Don't go talk to them yet, let it cool down, and then we will engage". They nodded, taking a deep breath to compose themselves. "I will, Top," they said. "I promise. I'll do whatever it takes to make things right."

And so, with the ARI's guidance, they set out to repair the damage that they had caused. They apologized to their old team and worked tirelessly to rebuild their trust in them. They were grateful to have been given the opportunity to make amends for their past mistakes.

The moral of both stories is simple: don't be a trash human, and make sure you have control over your Google and Apple Maps information. In the first story, the protagonist was a Marine Corps recruiter whose office phone number had been changed on both maps to the Army office next door, causing them to lose out on a significant number of potential contracts. In the second story, the protagonist was a Marine Corps recruiter who changed the phone number for their old office to one of their new recruiters, causing damage to their old team and their own reputation.

In both cases, the importance of correct contact information on Google and Apple maps was highlighted. It's a small but important detail that can have a big impact on their ability to reach and communicate with potential recruits.

So, to all recruiters out there, make sure you have control over your Google and Apple Maps information. It may seem like a minor issue, but it can make a big difference in your ability to reach and connect with potential recruits.

Reflection

It's important to have a strong online presence and to be easily accessible to potential recruits. That's where Google Maps and Apple Maps come in. According to a study by BrightLocal, a staggering 97% of consumers use online maps to find local businesses, with Google Maps being the most popular choice. This is further supported by a survey conducted by the Pew Research Center, which found that over 80% of adults in the United States use online maps to get directions or find businesses.

There are several benefits that Marine Corps recruiters can get from using Google Maps and Apple Maps listings. First and foremost, it allows potential recruits to easily find and contact your office. With just a few clicks, they can get directions, view your contact information, and even see pictures of your office. This can be especially useful for recruiters who are stationed in more rural or remote areas, where it might be harder for potential recruits to find them.

In addition to making it easier for potential recruits to find you, having a listing on Google Maps and Apple Maps can also help to increase the visibility and credibility of your office. When people search for businesses online, they often turn to maps to find what they're looking for. According to a survey conducted by BrightLocal, 88% of consumers trust online reviews as much as personal recommendations, which means that having positive reviews on your listing can help to build trust with potential recruits.

Finally, using Google Maps and Apple Maps can also help to improve your overall online presence and SEO. When you create a listing on these maps, you can add keywords and descriptions that can help to increase your visibility in search results. This can be especially useful for recruiters who want to reach potential recruits who are actively searching for information about joining the military.

To make the most of your Google Maps and Apple Maps listings, here are a few more detailed tips:

1. Make sure your information is accurate and up to date. This includes your office location, phone number, and hours of operation. Double-check that all this information is correct and update it if anything changes.

2. Add high-quality photos of your office to your listing. This can help potential recruits get a better sense of what your office looks like and what they can expect when they visit. Make sure to include a variety of photos that showcase different areas of your office, as well as any relevant amenities or features.

3. Use keywords and descriptions to help your listing show up in search results. Think about what potential recruits might be searching for when they look for military recruiters and use those keywords in your listing to increase your chances of being found. For example, you might include keywords like "military careers," "enlistment," or "veterans benefits."

4. Encourage your satisfied recruits and parents to leave reviews on your listing. Positive reviews can help to build credibility and trust with potential recruits. Consider sending out a request for reviews to your past clients or offering incentives for them to leave a review.

Even making it a part of the Sunday Shipper routine is a good idea.

5. Respond to any negative reviews or feedback you receive. This can show potential recruits that you take their concerns seriously and are willing to address any issues they may have. Be sure to thank them for their feedback and provide a clear and helpful response to any concerns they raise.

By following these tips, you can make your Google Maps and Apple Maps listings even more effective in reaching and attracting potential prospects.

Discord – Not Just for Gamers

Anecdote – Gaming Apps in Restaurants

I was always on the lookout for ways to streamline my processes and make my job easier. That's why, when my wife and I walked into a small business to pick up an order we had placed, I was immediately drawn to the app the cashier was using at the counter. I had heard of Discord before, but only in the context of it being a popular communication tool among gamers. So, when I saw it being used in a business setting, I was curious to learn more.

As I spoke with the cashier, she explained that the business used Discord to pass information back and forth, from orders being placed to paid time off requests. It was a convenient and efficient way to communicate, and she said it had greatly improved their operations.

I was intrigued by this idea and immediately thought of my own recruiting office. I knew that my friend Juan, a fellow recruiter, would be interested in this as well. So when I got back to the office, I told him about the app and how it was being used in this small business.

Juan was just as interested as I was and decided to ask his poolees about their experiences with Discord. To our surprise, almost every member of the delayed entry program in our pool told us that they already used Discord on a regular basis. It was a popular tool among young people, and it seemed like it could be a valuable resource for our recruiting efforts as well.

Juan and I decided to give Discord a try. We used it to pass along information about events and functions, take accountability, and share ideas. It quickly became an invaluable resource, making it much easier for us to communicate and stay organized.

Reflection

Discord is a communication platform designed specifically for online communities and teams. It offers a variety of features including voice and text chat, screen sharing, and the ability to create and join multiple channels within a server. Discord is particularly popular among gamers, but it has also gained widespread use among a variety of other communities, including businesses, schools, and organizations.

According to a study conducted by the Pew Research Center, over half (75%) of all teenagers in the United States use Discord. This makes it an especially popular tool among high school students, who are often the target demographic for Marine Corps recruitment efforts. In addition, a survey conducted by SuperData Research found that Discord had more than 100 million monthly active users as of 2018, with most users being between the ages of 18 and 24.

As a Marine Corps recruiter, managing the DEP can be a challenging and time-consuming task. It's important to stay organized and efficiently communicate with recruits in order to ensure that they are prepared for boot camp and their future careers as Marines. That's where Discord comes in.

By using Discord, or a similar group messaging app such as Slack, recruiters can create a dedicated channel for their DEP where they can share important information, answer questions, and stay in touch with poolees. This can save time and make it easier to stay organized, as all communication is centralized in one place. In fact, a study by the Harvard Business Review found that teams that use communication tools like Discord are more likely to operate efficiently and effectively. Another study by the University of Southern California found that teams that use group messaging apps, like Discord, have higher levels of team cohesion and collaboration compared to teams that do not use these tools.

Here are nine basic tips for building a successful Discord or group messaging channel for your DEP:

1. Create separate channels for different types of information. For example, you might have a general channel for announcements and a

separate channel for questions and answers.

2. Use Discord's tagging and notification system to ensure that important messages reach the right people.

3. Make use of Discord's screen-sharing feature to give presentations or demonstrations.

4. Set up role-based permissions to ensure that only authorized individuals have access to certain channels or information.

5. Use Discord's integrations with other tools, such as Google Calendar, to keep track of events and appointments.

6. Use Discord's text formatting options to make messages more visually appealing and easy to read.

7. Encourage recruits to share their own experiences and ideas in the channel.

8. Use Discord's analytics and reporting features to track activity and engagement in the channel.

9. Stay active and responsive in the channel to build trust and maintain strong relationships with recruits.

You can create a dynamic and effective Discord channel for your DEP that will help you stay organized and communicate more efficiently with your Poolees if you invest in the platfor. In the end, this will help you better prepare them for their future careers as Marines and ensure the success of your Pool Program, just make sure to update their Pool Cards.

Use TextRecruit to Screen Lists

Anecdote – How I Found Initial Success in My Second Tour

Back in March of 2023, I found myself on a second recruiting tour. This time I volunteered because I did not really enjoy Camp Lejeune, the bonus was nice, and I did not have a deployment coming up for at least two years. I was assigned to a recruiting office in Aurora, CO, faced with an overwhelming challenge. The office had been underperforming for seven months straight, missing our mission targets every single time. The morale was low, the recruiters felt dispirited, and the pressure from higher up was becoming unbearable. But I knew something had to change. I could not change the toxic work culture from higher but I could make the job a little bit easier for my Marines.

As the new SNCOIC, I realized that part of our problem wasn't lack of effort but the outdated approach we were using. The reliance on traditional recruitment techniques such as cold-calling, high school presentations, and local job fairs seemed to have hit a wall. We were swimming against the current, and it was time to turn the tide.

I decided to leverage a technology that would transform our outreach strategy. I dusted off a program that nobody in the station was using called TextRecruit. The program allowed us to text thousands of leads with the click of a button. People did not believe in the program because it had not proved useful in the past, but I believed the value of the response is equal to the value of the message you send. My question was, how in 2023 are we still just calling random numbers on a list? So my goal was to use TextRecruit to filter out all the hostile and highly disinterested people on the list so I could give my team real people to answer the phone.

On recruiting we generally have two types of lists. First, high school lists that are filled predominantly with parents' numbers. Cold calling these numbers usually led to unanswered calls or disinterested conversations. To change this, our TextRecruit campaign to the high school lists aimed to obtain direct numbers for the students. We initiated a text campaign explaining who we were and the purpose of our communication, seeking permission to directly contact their children. Surprisingly, the responses were moistly positive and yielded better results than previous attempts by the RS.

The second types of lists are from community colleges, which comprised mostly direct numbers, but our challenge was engaging their interest. Our TextRecruit campaign to these lists was designed to pique interest and find out who was willing to talk. We framed our messages with enticing narratives about the Marine Corps, focusing on opportunities for personal and professional growth, educational benefits, and the honor of serving their country. I'm currently authoring an addition to this book filled with scripts for you to use..

By running campaigns and always using drip messages, the TextRecruit program allowed us to reach a larger audience, track responses, and filter out interested candidates. The traditional telephone calls didn't stop, but their purpose was to screen out the people who were willing to answer the phone. We stopped blindly dialing numbers, this way we could focus our efforts on those who had already shown a spark of interest.

The results were astounding. Within the first two months of implementing TextRecruit, our office began to witness a substantial improvement. By the third month, not only did we hit our mission, but we started overwriting. It was a breakthrough that injected a newfound energy into the entire office. More importantly, it brought back the belief in our ability to accomplish our mission.

In this digital age, we need to continually evolve our strategies and harness the power of technology to improve our recruitment process. Our experience with TextRecruit underscores the importance of innovation in addressing challenges. The journey from underperforming to overwriting demonstrated that technology, when used effectively, could serve as a formidable tool in the hands of a Marine Corps recruiter.

Reflection

One of the primary takeaways from our transformative experience was understanding the power of technology in refining our recruitment process. Any software or program, like TextRecruit, that helps filter down your list to people who will genuinely engage, can be a game-changer. The tool you select may vary based on your particular needs and the demographics you're working with, but the underlying principle remains the same.

The goal is to use technology to automate the initial stages of outreach, allowing you to spend more time with the individuals who have shown interest. Remember, it's not about replacing the human touch in recruitment; rather, it's about enabling it to be more focused, more personalized, and more efficient.

Now, the challenge is to be creative and innovative in your approach. Don't limit yourself to the strategies that we used, but take them as a starting point to develop your own techniques. Perhaps there's another program out there better suited to your needs, or maybe you'll find a way to leverage social media platforms or other digital tools to reach your target audience. The key is to stay adaptable and receptive to new methods.

In this line of work, time is the essence, and how you use it can make or break your success. By filtering your list down to the individuals who are more likely to answer your calls and engage with your message, you free up time to focus on those who have already made the commitment: your Poolees.

In fact, once you master the art of generating two Prospect Applicant Cards in an hour, you can dedicate the rest of your time to developing your Poolees. Nurturing these relationships is essential not only for maintaining their commitment but also for fostering a sense of camaraderie, belonging, and morale among them. This concentrated attention reduces the chances of apathy and discharges, ensuring a steady stream of committed and engaged recruits.

Remember that effective recruiting is a blend of smart strategy, efficient tools, and personalized attention. Harness technology to streamline your initial outreach, focus on those who display genuine interest, and invest your time in nurturing and developing your Poolees. Be open to innovation, be adaptable, and above all, remember that at the heart of every successful recruitment effort is a genuine connection between recruiter and recruit.

3 ON HIGH SCHOOLS

Chapter Introduction

I never expected to end up in Marin Coun5ty, California. As a Marine, I was used to being placed in different locations. I had been deployed to some of the most violent countries in the world, and I was no stranger to hostility. But the hostility I faced in Marin County was on another level.

Growing up, I hadn't had the opportunity to live in a predominantly white neighborhood. In fact, I was one of only three white kids in my graduating class of almost 500 students. So, being thrown into a county where the majority of the population was white and wealthy was a bit of a culture shock for me.

It was 2018, and Donald Trump was the President. As a member of the military, I tried to steer away from politics every chance I could, but I couldn't deny that the tension in the air was palpable. I had always known that not everyone was a fan of the military, but the high schools in Marin County took it to a whole new level. They made it known that they did not like the military and gave me almost zero access to their students.

During my first week on recruiting duty, I was checking out a part of the county called Sausalito. As I walked down the street, an old woman spat on me and called me a "baby killer." I was taken aback by the venom in her voice and the contempt in her eyes. I never expected it, especially not from an elderly woman. The people around didn't say anything either, some even seemed to agree with what she did.

It was frustrating, to say the least. I had always been passionate about my job and about recruiting young men and women to serve their country. But in Marin County, it felt like an uphill battle. I wasn't used to being shut out and disregarded like this.

But I was determined to make the best of it. I set up shop in my small office on the outskirts of town and began reaching out to the high schools, trying to find any way possible to get in front of potential recruits. It wasn't easy, but I was determined to make a difference and show Marin County's people that the military was more than just a political talking point.

Despite the initial challenges and hostility that I faced in Marin County, I was eventually able to turn things around. It wasn't easy, and it took a lot of hard work and persistence, but I was able to gain access to a huge swath of the student body in my priority schools.

I started by connecting with teachers outside of the school. I attended school board meetings, introduced myself at PTA meetings, and made myself a regular presence in the schools. I was determined to show the people of Marin County that I was more than just a recruiter, that I was a member of the community, and that I cared about the students and their future.

I began to listen to the concerns and reservations of the teachers and community members, and I worked to address their fears and questions. I knew that many of them hated the military and were worried about the dangers of military service and the potential for their students to be sent into harm's way. So, I made a point to be honest about the dangers and emphasize the various career options available in the military, and I talked about the extensive training and support that was provided to all service members.

One of the keys to gaining the trust of the teachers and community members in Marin County was being honest and upfront about my quota and enlistment practices. I knew that many of them had concerns about the military's recruitment tactics and about the pressure that recruiters often faced meeting their quotas. So, I was transparent about my goals and about the fact that I was under pressure to enlist a certain number of students. I told them I have a job to do but I would always put the student's best interest at the forefront.

I also made sure to be upfront about the enlistment process and the various options available to the students. I provided them with all the necessary information and resources, and I made it clear that the decision to join the military was entirely up to them.

This honesty and transparency went a long way in gaining the trust of the teachers and community members. They appreciated my honesty and my commitment to the students, and it helped to build strong, positive relationships with them. As a result, I was able to gain a lot more access to the student body and to have more meaningful conversations with them about their futures and their potential in the military.

It wasn't easy, and I faced a lot of skepticism and resistance along the way. But I refused to give up. I knew that if I could just get in front of the students, if I could just speak to them and share my experiences, then I could help them see the value of military service.

Eventually, my persistence paid off. I was able to start giving class talks and getting lists of students who were interested in learning more about the military. It was a huge accomplishment, and I was thrilled to finally connect with the students and share my passion for military service with them.

Over time, I was able to build strong relationships with teachers and school administrators, and I became a regular presence in the schools. It was rewarding to see the students respond to my message and to see them start to consider military service as a viable option for their future.

I knew that I still had a lot of work to do, and that there would always be those who opposed the military and what it stood for. But I was determined to keep working hard and to keep trying to reach as many students as possible. I knew that if I could just help a few of them see the value of military service and the opportunities it could provide, then it would all be worth it.

Prior to getting involved in the schools in Marin County, the county was producing less than one enlistment every two months. It was clear that the military was not a popular or well-respected institution in the community, and that the students lacked interest in military service.

However, after getting involved with the schools and working to build relationships with the teachers, administrators, and students, I was able to turn things around. I averaged 3.6 enlistments per month, and I was able to make a significant impact on the lives of the young men and women in the county.

The moral of the story is that even in challenging locations if you make use of your high school and community college program, you can find success.□

What To Ask for From Your Schools

Anecdote – You Get What You Ask For

I've learned that you often get what you ask for from your high schools. If you go in there and just ask for a meeting with a teacher, that's typically what you'll get. But if you ask for a meeting with the Superintendent of the school district, you'll be surprised at how often you can get that as well. I had a lot of success and a lot of failure in my role as a recruiter, and I've found that when I did succeed it was often because I was willing to ask for what I needed. When I first started working in Marin County, I knew that I needed more access to the student body if I was going to be successful in my job. So, I started asking for more.

I asked for meetings with teachers, and I was able to establish strong relationships with many of them. I asked for meetings with the Superintendent, and I was able to have some valuable conversations about the military and its role in the community. I asked to speak to one class a semester, and I was able to share my experiences and knowledge with the students.

I even asked for my own office, and while I didn't get that, I did get my own desk in one of the school's counseling offices. It may not have been my own private space, but it was a step in the right direction, and it gave me a place to work and meet with students.

I've learned that if you just ask for what you need, you'll be surprised at how often you can get it. Of course, you need to be respectful and professional in your requests, but if you're willing to put in the effort and make a strong case for why you need something, you'll often find that people are willing to help.

However, I've also learned that sometimes you don't get exactly what you ask for, but you can still achieve your goals with a little bit of flexibility and persistence. When I first started working in Marin County, I asked to be a "guest lecturer" for one day a semester in every 12th-grade class. Seemed like a big ask, and while I didn't get exactly what I wanted, I was still able to schedule at least one class talk a week in some capacity by being flexible and open to other opportunities.

If you are willing to work with the schools and the teachers, you can find ways to get in front of the students and share your experiences and knowledge with them. I wasn't always able to speak to every class, but I was able to reach a significant number of students by being proactive and finding ways to connect with them.

Reflection

There are three things that I believe we should be asking for from our schools. First and foremost, we should be asking for the opportunity to give one class talk to each 12th and 11th-grade class per semester. This is a crucial way to connect with the students and share our experiences and knowledge with them. By speaking to the students directly, we can help to answer their questions, address their concerns, and inspire them to consider military service as a viable option for their future.

Second, we should be asking for complete lists of students. Some schools are reluctant to give this up (I know the schools I worked in were). But besides being mandated by law, it will allow you to track the students who are interested in the military and to reach out to them directly. It will also give you the opportunity to connect with students who may not have otherwise considered military service and to provide them with the information and resources they need to make an informed decision.

Finally, we should be asking for an office in the school with the ability to pull kids out of class to screen them for enlistment. This will give us a dedicated space to meet with students and conduct the necessary screening and evaluation processes. It will also allow us to work more closely with the school and establish a stronger presence in the community. Now I know asking for your own space in the school seems like a huge request, but it is only a big thing if you make it a big thing. They are government workers the same as you are, it is not their personal space but rather the property of the government. Ask for it, the worst they can say is no, and by bringing up the question you have moved it from something that is way out of bounds, to a request that is just a little bit out of bounds.

In addition to asking for these three things from our schools, it's also important to be open to finding ways to "get to yes" when faced with resistance or objections. Nobody wants to be the person who says no, and often there may be alternative solutions or compromises that can be reached.

For a little more help here are ten ways to get what you want out of your assigned high schools.

1. Clearly define what you want: Before you start asking for things, it's important to have a clear understanding of what it is you want. This will help you to be more specific in your requests and to make a stronger case for why you need something.

2. Do your research: It's important to have a solid understanding of the situation and the needs of the people you are asking for

something from. This will help you to tailor your requests and to present a more compelling case for why you need something i.e., knowing about an unused desk somewhere in the school would be a great thing to know before asking for one.

3. Be respectful and professional: It's important to always be respectful and professional in your requests, even if you are facing resistance or skepticism. This will help you to establish positive relationships and to gain the trust of those you are asking for something from.

4. Make a strong case: When making your request, be sure to clearly articulate why you need something and how it will benefit both you and the person you are asking. This will help to strengthen your argument and to make your request more compelling.

5. Be flexible and open to compromise: While it's important to be clear about what you want, it's also important to be open to compromise and to be willing to find alternative solutions. This will help you to build stronger relationships and to find common ground with those you are asking for something from.

6. Build relationships: Establishing strong relationships with those you are asking for something from can go a long way in helping you to get what you want. Take the time to get to know people, listen to their concerns, and work to establish trust and understanding.

7. Be persistent: If you are met with resistance or if your request is not immediately granted, don't give up. Be persistent and continue to follow up and advocate for what you want.

8. Look for alternative avenues: If you are having difficulty getting what you want through traditional channels, consider looking for alternative avenues. This might involve seeking out resources or contacts within the community or finding creative ways to get your message out.

9. Be willing to put in the effort: Gaining what you want often requires hard work and effort. Be prepared to put in the time and energy needed to make your case and achieve your goals.

10. Keep a positive attitude: Finally, it's important to maintain a positive attitude and stay focused on your goals. This will help you to stay motivated and to stay committed to your vision, even when faced with challenges or setbacks.

McKenzie's Binder Idea

Anecdote – A Story About All-Hands

I sat in the cramped auditorium near the recruiting station with a sense of frustration and boredom. The monthly "all hands" training was always a tedious affair, with seemingly endless presentations and updates that seemed to drag on for hours. I checked my phone every few minutes, hoping that time would somehow speed up and this interminable training would be over soon.

And while there were a few moments of praise for those who had excelled, most of the day felt like it was spent shaming those who had underperformed. I was empathetic for my fellow recruiters as they were called out for their mistakes and shortcomings. But at the same time, I was grateful that I had managed to avoid the same fate.

As the hours ticked by, my mind began to wander. I found myself daydreaming about all the things I could be doing instead of sitting in this stuffy conference room. I simply did not want to be there, thought it was a waste of my time, and wanted to spend time with my family.

The next class began. The speaker was a seasoned career recruiter named Thomas McKenzie, a man who was known for his ability to sell just about anything. This man could sell ice to an Eskimo. He had a combover hairstyle that was always out of regulation, and a mind that seemed to be constantly plotting and scheming. He was a smart, calculated, man who genuinely cared about his team.

Thomas began his presentation by discussing the importance of building relationships with high schools. He brought out a binder as an example, which was white with the logos of the school and the Marine Corps emblazoned on the cover. The school's name and the local recruiting office's phone number were also prominently displayed. The binder was meant to have all information in it that a high school needed about the Marine Corps.

As Thomas spoke, the rest of the class seemed impressed by his charisma and enthusiasm. He had a way of making everything sound important and worth considering, and I found a few of my fellow recruiters hanging on his every word.

"The key is to get these binders into the hands of every decision-maker at the school," Thomas explained. "It's something physical that they can reference anytime they have a question, and it's just another reminder of your presence in their office."

But as much as I tried to focus on Thomas's presentation, I found my mind wandering. I had heard all this before, and to be honest, I didn't see the point in putting in the extra effort to create personalized binders for each school. It seemed like a lot of work for something that might not even make a difference in my recruitment efforts.

So, I sat back in my chair and let Thomas's words wash over me, not bothering to take any notes. I figured I could just wing it and hope for the best. After all, I had been successful in the past without going to such lengths. Why bother with all the extra work now?

But as the presentation went on, Thomas was clearly passionate about this approach, and he had some convincing arguments in his favor. Maybe I should have paid more attention and at least given his ideas a chance.

Even though I didn't see much value in the personalized binder approach, I decided to give it a shot with one school. I figured that if it didn't work out, I could at least say I tried. So, I took the time to create a good-looking binder, filled with all sorts of information about the Marine Corps and its value to the school.

I was proud of the finished product, and I made my way over to one of my priority schools, binder in hand, and headed straight for the principal's office. To my surprise, the principal was impressed by the binder. They flipped through the pages, taking in all the information, and thanked me for taking the time to put it together. I left the school feeling hopeful that this approach might work, and I couldn't wait to see the results.

It wasn't until much later, after I had left the recruiting station and moved on to PCS back to the fleet, that I learned the true impact of that single binder. A recruiter who used to work for me told me that they had sent seven teachers to the Educator's workshop that year, all because the principal had read about it in the binder I had dropped off.

I was surprised by this revelation and couldn't help but wonder how much more success I could have had if I had made the effort to create binders for each of my priority schools. Who knows how many contracts were generated by the attendance of those seven educators at the workshop?

Reflection

I have learned the importance of building relationships with high schools. And one effective way I have found to do this is by dropping off personalized binders like the one Thomas told me about. These binders are filled with information about the Marine Corps and its value to the school community, and they can be a great resource for both students and teachers.

So, what should Marine Corps recruiters put in these binders before they distribute them? PDF and Word files can be found on my website, but here are a few suggestions:

1. Educators workshop: One of the key pieces of information to include in the binder is information on the Educator's workshop. This workshop is a great opportunity for teachers to learn more about the Marine Corps and the opportunities it offers to students. By highlighting this workshop in the binder, you can help encourage teachers to attend and learn more about the Marine Corps.

2. Enlistment options: Another important piece of information to include in the binder is information on enlistment options. Students and their families may have questions about the different ways to join the Marine Corps, and the binder is a great place to provide this information.

3. Post 9-11 GI Bill: Another important piece of information to include in the binder is information on the Post 9-11 GI Bill. This program provides financial assistance to military personnel and their families, and it can be a powerful incentive for students to consider joining the Marine Corps.

4. Classroom presentations: Advertise that you are willing and ready to take over a 12th or 11th-grade class for a day. Tell them what topics you can cover and how to schedule you. This gives the teacher a chance to catch up on administrative work, and it allows you to present information about the Marine Corps to the students.

5. Contact information: It's also important to include phone numbers and contact information for the recruiting office in the binder. This makes it easy for the staff members to get in touch with

you if they have any questions or want to further discuss the marine corps.

6. Social media links: In today's digital age, it's important to have a strong online presence. That's why you should also include links to your recruiting office's social media accounts in the binder. This allows students and teachers to connect with you and stay updated on the latest news and information from the marine corps.

7. USMAP: Another important piece of information to include in the binder is information on USMAP. This program provides technical training and hands-on experience to Marine Corps personnel, and it can be a valuable resource for students who are interested in pursuing a career in the military.

8. Marine Corps Band: Finally, my former XO would kill me if I didn't include this. You should include information on the Marine Corps Band in the binder.

Marine Corps recruiters should make the effort to create and distribute personalized binders like the one Thomas told me about. These binders are a great way to build relationships with high schools and provide students and teachers with valuable information about the marine corps. By including information on the Educators workshop, enlistment options, the Post 9-11 GI Bill, classroom presentations, contact information, social media links, USMAP, and the Marine Corps Band, you can help ensure that you are making the most of your recruitment efforts.

So, you have the binders made but who are these decision-makers? In most high schools, they are typically the principal, assistant principals, and guidance counselors. These are the individuals who have the most influence on the school's policies and procedures, and they are the ones whom you will want to focus on when it comes to building relationships.

How do you go about getting a meeting with these decision-makers? One of the most effective ways is to simply reach out to them and request a meeting. You can do this by emailing or calling their office, messaging them on LinkedIn, or by stopping by in person if you are in the area. Be sure to explain the purpose of the meeting, which is to drop off a personalized binder about the Marine Corps, and include a reason why it needs to be in person. A good reason for this is to see if there are ways you and the principal can develop a mutually beneficial relationship. This will give them a clear idea of what to expect, and it will help everyone get the most out of their meetings.

Another tip is to be professional and respectful in all your interactions with the decision-makers. Remember, you are representing the Marine Corps, and it's important to make a good impression. So be punctual, wear your uniform, and be respectful of their time and schedules. It's important to remember that as a Marine Corps recruiter, you do not need to be timid when dealing with teachers, principals, or even the superintendent. While it's important to be respectful, you should also remember that you are a member of the United States Marine Corps, and you have nothing to feel intimidated by when it comes to high school staff.

Instead, speak to them as equals. Remember that you are both working towards the same goal of helping students succeed and that you have a valuable perspective to offer. By speaking to them with confidence and respect, you will likely find that they will reciprocate in kind.

So don't be afraid to assert yourself and make your presence known. You have a valuable role to play in the high school community, and you deserve to be treated with the same respect as anyone else.

□

Class Talks

Anecdote One – My First Class Talk

I was nervous as I stood in front of the class at Novato High School, giving my first-ever presentation as a Marine Corps recruiter. I had spent hours rehearsing and practicing my speech, but now that I was actually in front of the students, I was a little anxious.

Despite my nerves, I managed to get through my pre-rehearsed class, which lasted for about 30 minutes. I talked about the various opportunities available in the Marine Corps, including training, education, and travel. I also touched on the importance of leadership, teamwork, and discipline, and how serving in the military can help young people develop these valuable skills.

As I neared the end of my presentation, I felt a mix of relief and excitement as I prepared to open the floor for questions. My heart raced as I scanned the room, looking for raised hands. A few students were quick to respond, and I called on them one by one, feeling a sense of nervous anticipation as I waited for their questions.

The first student asked where I had served in the military, I responded that I had been deployed to a variety of places including Iraq, Kuwait, Japan, Australia, Korea, and various small islands in the Pacific region, I couldn't help but notice the looks of awe and admiration on some of the students' faces. It was a privilege to be able to share my experiences with the next generation and to be able to inspire them to consider a similar path. And as I finished answering the student's question and moved on to the next, I couldn't wait to see what else the class had in store for me.

I stood in front of the class, fielding questions from the students and was caught off guard when one student raised their hand and asked, "How can you serve in the military while Donald Trump is president?"

I must admit, I felt a little agitated by the question. As a member of the military, I had sworn to support and defend the Constitution of the United States of America, and to obey the orders of the President of the United States of America, regardless of my personal feelings or beliefs. I had served under President Obama as well as President Trump, and I had always done so faithfully because the beautiful thing about the military is that it is non-partisan.

But despite my initial irritation, I knew that I had to answer the student's question honestly and professionally. So, taking a deep breath, I explained that my duty as a member of the military was to serve my country and uphold the values of the United States, no matter who was in office. I also emphasized that the military was a place where people of all backgrounds and beliefs could come together to serve a common cause and that it was important to remember that we were all on the same team, working towards a common goal.

I was relieved when the student didn't ask a follow-up question, and I ended my presentation by saying that if any students had further questions or were interested in learning more about the Marine Corps, they could come to talk to me after class.

As I packed up my things and prepared to leave the classroom, I felt disappointed as I realized that only one student had stayed behind to speak with me after my presentation. While I had thought my presentation had gone well at the time, looking back on it now, I had missed a huge opportunity to connect with the students and share my knowledge and experiences with them.

One of the biggest mistakes I made was not capturing any data on the students in the class. I didn't get their names or contact information, so I had no way to follow up with them or keep in touch. This meant that I had no way to track the impact of my presentation or to see if any of the students were interested in learning more about the Marine Corps.

In addition to not capturing any data, I also didn't give a strong call to action or schedule a follow-up meeting with the teacher. I simply told the students that they could come to talk to me if they had any questions or were interested in learning more, but I didn't give them a specific reason to do so or a clear next step. This meant that I missed out on the opportunity to engage with the students and provide them with more information and resources to help them make informed decisions about their futures.

I knew that my presentation had been a missed opportunity, and I knew that I needed to do better next time. But the last class talk I ever did was vastly better than the first.

Anecdote Two – My Last Class Talk

The last class talk I ever gave was at Jesse Bethel High School in Vallejo, California, just a few weeks before the COVID-19 pandemic shut everything down. I was covering a talk for one of my recruiters who was dealing with an applicant. The teacher invited my recruiter to speak to his class. The teacher taught English and graciously offered to let us speak to every one of his classes for the entire day so he could catch up on grading papers. The teacher and I had gone out for coffee and lunch several times at this point, and we knew each other well.

I arrived at the school about an hour before the first class was set to start, eager to get everything set up. I had brought a box of coffee from Starbucks to help me make it through the day, and I also offered some to the teacher if he wanted any. We chatted for a few minutes about how his day was going and how his students were doing before I set up my PowerPoint presentation on the screen.

I spent a lot of time putting together the presentation, carefully selecting photos and anecdotes from my time in the Middle East and the Pacific region to share with the students. My goal was to give them a sense of what it was like to serve in the military and how the skills and experiences they gained could benefit them in their future careers, whether they chose to join the military or pursue a different path.

As I started my first presentation of the day, I could feel the energy in the room shift as the students became more focused and engaged. I began by introducing myself and sharing a little bit about my background and my experiences in the military. I talked about the various opportunities available in the Marine Corps, including training, education, and travel, as well as the importance of leadership, teamwork, and discipline.

I neared the end of my introduction and was excited as I prepared to delve into the focus of my presentation: intelligence writing. I knew that this was an area that would parallel a lot of the things the students were learning, and I wanted to make sure I gave them a comprehensive overview of how their English skills could be applied in the military.

I started by explaining the importance of clear and concise communication in the military, particularly when it came to intelligence writing. I shared examples of how being able to effectively convey information and ideas could make a huge difference in the success of a mission, and how attention to detail was crucial in this type of work. I made it a point to constantly probe the audience to ensure they were following along and staying engaged.

Next, I talked about the role of critical thinking and analysis in intelligence writing. I used a video and explained how being able to analyze and interpret complex information, and draw logical conclusions based on that information, was a key skill in the military. I shared some of my own experiences in this regard, and how the skills I had developed in my English classes had helped me excel in my military career.

As I finished my presentation, I opened the floor for questions. I was always happy to answer any questions the students had, as I believed it was important to be as transparent and honest as possible about my experiences in the military.

A few students raised their hands, and I called on them one by one. The first student asked about my deployment to the Middle East, and I shared some stories and insights about what it was like to serve in that part of the world. The second student asked about the training and education opportunities available in the Marine Corps, and I gave a detailed overview of the various programs and resources available to help service members grow and develop in their careers.

Throughout the day, I gave a total of five presentations, each one slightly different than the last as I tailored my message to the specific needs and interests of each class. I talked about the various career options available in the military, and how the skills and experiences gained in the military could translate to success in the civilian world. I also talked about the importance of teamwork and leadership, and how serving in the military could help young people develop these valuable skills.

At the end of each presentation, I included a QR code that linked to a Google Form for the students to fill out with their name, grade, phone number, address, age, and a multiple-choice question asking what they planned to do after graduation. I knew that this was a great way to capture data on the students and gauge their interest in the military as a potential career option.

That day of presentations resulted in the collection of 126 student data, 15 appointments set for the next two weeks, and a lot of engagement. It was a vast improvement from the first class talk I gave almost three years prior.

Reflection

Giving a great classroom presentation is not always easy, and it takes careful planning and execution to make it a success.

One of the most important things to remember when giving a classroom presentation is to be authentic and relevant to the students. This means that you need to be genuine and open about your experiences in the military, and you need to talk about things that are relevant to the students' lives and interests. A good example of this is to give a class on what you do in the military, and how it relates to the student's future goals and aspirations.

Another key element of a great classroom presentation is to bring media to the presentation. A photo or video is worth a thousand words, and it can help to engage and captivate the students in a way that simply talking can't. If you just talk the whole time, it can be boring and not very engaging, so make sure to mix things up by using a variety of media to illustrate your points.

Another tip for giving a great classroom presentation is to make it a story. As the saying goes, "facts tell, stories sell," and this is especially true when it comes to engaging the students. By sharing stories and anecdotes from your experiences in the military, you can help to bring your presentation to life and make it more relatable and interesting for the students.

A fourth tip for giving a great classroom presentation is to ask to present to every one of the teacher's classes, rather than just one. This will give you the opportunity to reach more students and make a bigger impact. It can also help to build your credibility and expertise, as the teacher will see that you are committed to making the most of your time with their students.

Building strong relationships with the teachers who teach seniors, such as 12th-grade English teachers, government teachers, economics teachers, and calculus teachers is critical. These teachers are often the ones who are most influential in helping students decide what to do after graduation and having a strong relationship with them can be a huge asset. By taking the time to get to know these teachers and to understand their needs and priorities, you can more effectively tailor your presentations to meet their needs and the needs of their students.

Perhaps the most important thing to do during a classroom presentation is capturing data on the students. One way to do this is by using a QR code that links to a Google Form where the students can fill out their name, grade, phone number, address, age, and a multiple-choice question asking what they plan to do after graduation. Capturing this data can be incredibly valuable for tracking the effectiveness of your presentations and for follow-up outreach to students who are interested in learning more about the military.

Giving a great classroom presentation to high school students is all about authenticity, relevance, media, storytelling, building relationships, and capturing data. By following these tips, you can make your presentations more engaging and effective, and you can better connect with the next generation of potential recruits.

In addition to the tips above here are a few ways to give a better presentation as a canvassing recruiter:

1. Start by identifying your audience and what they want to learn. This will help you tailor your presentation to their needs and interests.

2. Use a variety of media, including photos, videos, and other visuals, to illustrate your points and keep your audience engaged.

3. Use storytelling to make your presentation more engaging and memorable. Share anecdotes and examples to help illustrate your points.

4. Practice your presentation beforehand to make sure you are comfortable and confident when giving it.

5. Use clear, concise language and avoid using jargon or technical terms that your audience may not understand.

6. Engage with your audience by asking questions and encouraging participation.

7. Use props or demonstrations to make your presentation more interactive and hands-on.

8. Use clear, easy-to-read slides with minimal text and plenty of graphics.

9. End your presentation with a clear call to action, such as inviting the audience to ask questions or encouraging them to follow up with you for more information.

It's All About the Data

Anecdote – A Look at Data Collection in Politics

In the early 1990s, the internet was still a relatively new and unfamiliar concept to most people. While it had been around for a few decades, it was only in the mid-90s that it began to gain widespread mainstream adoption. This was particularly true in the United States, where the number of people with internet access had grown significantly in the years leading up to the 1996 presidential election.

One of the key players in this election was Bill Clinton, who was running for re-election as President of the United States. Clinton was a savvy politician who was well-versed in the latest technology and was always looking for ways to use it to his advantage. As such, he saw the internet as a powerful tool that could be used to connect with voters, raise money, and spread his message.

To this end, Clinton's campaign team set up a website called "Bill Clinton for President," which was designed to serve as a central hub for all the campaign's online activities. The site was loaded with information about Clinton's policies and positions, as well as updates on his campaign events and activities. It also provided a platform for supporters to connect with one another and share their own thoughts and ideas about the campaign.

In addition to the campaign website, Clinton's team also made extensive use of email to communicate with voters and supporters. They used this medium to send out regular updates about the campaign, as well as to solicit donations and volunteer support. Clinton's campaign was one of the first to fully embrace the power of email, and it played a significant role in helping him to build a strong base of support.

One particularly innovative aspect of Clinton's email strategy was the use of personalized emails. By gathering data about the interests and concerns of individual voters, the campaign was able to send targeted messages that were specifically tailored to the needs and interests of each recipient. This helped to build a sense of connection and engagement with voters and contributed to the campaign's success.

Another key aspect of Clinton's online strategy was the use of data collection and analysis. His campaign team used a variety of tools and techniques to track the online behavior of voters, to better understand their interests and concerns. This data was then used to tailor the campaign's messaging and outreach efforts to better resonate with specific demographics and voting blocs.

One example of this was the campaign's use of targeted online advertising. By analyzing data about the online habits of voters, Clinton's team was able to identify the websites and platforms that were most popular with certain groups of people. They then used this information to place targeted ads on these sites, to reach these voters with messages that were specifically tailored to them.

In addition to targeting ads, Clinton's campaign also used data analysis to optimize the design and content of its website. By tracking the way that visitors interacted with the site, the team was able to identify the features and pages that were most popular and make changes to improve the overall user experience.

Clinton's use of the internet and data collection played a key role in his successful re-election campaign in 1996. By using these tools to connect with voters, raise money, and spread his message, he was able to effectively reach a wide audience and build a strong base of support. His innovative approach to using technology in politics set a precedent that has been followed by many politicians in the years since.

Reflection

As a Marine Corps recruiter, it is important to collect data when you give class presentations for a variety of reasons. By gathering this information, you can more effectively identify which students you have talked to, re-contact those students you presented to, and obtain direct cell phone numbers for students on your lists.

First and foremost, collecting data during your class presentations will help you to identify which students you have talked to. This is particularly important because you may be giving presentations to multiple classes at different schools, and it can be difficult to keep track of all the students you have spoken to. By collecting data on the students, you can create a database of names and contact information that you can refer to when you need to follow up with potential recruits.

In addition to helping you identify which students you have talked to, collecting data during your class presentations will also allow you to re-contact those students you presented to. This can be particularly useful if you want to follow up with students who seemed interested in joining the military or if you want to send them additional information about the Marine Corps. By having this data, you can easily reach out to students via email or phone to provide them with more information or to schedule a meeting.

Collecting data during your class presentations will allow you to obtain direct cell phone numbers for students on your lists. This is important because it gives you a direct way to communicate with potential recruits and to keep them updated on events or opportunities related to the Marine Corps. By having direct cell phone numbers, you can more easily follow up with students and ensure that they are receiving the information they need to make an informed decision about their future. This solves an issue discussed about in a previous chapter, most high school lists having only parent phone numbers.

Collecting data during your class presentations is an essential aspect of being a Marine Corps recruiter. By gathering information on the students you have spoken to, you can more effectively identify, re-contact, and communicate with potential recruits. Whether you are following up with students who seemed interested in joining the military or sending them additional information about the Marine Corps, having accurate and up-to-date data is crucial to the success of your recruitment efforts. So next time you give a class presentation, make sure to take the time to collect data on the students you have talked to. This simple step can have a big impact on your ability to connect with and engage potential recruits, and it can ultimately lead to a more successful recruitment process for the Marine Corps.

As a pro tip, I strongly encourage the use of digital forms instead of paper ones for class talks. There are several reasons why a digital survey is more valuable than a paper survey. First and foremost, digital surveys are more convenient for both the surveyor and the survey taker. Because they can be accessed online, digital surveys can be completed from any device with an internet connection, which makes it easy for respondents to complete them at their own convenience. This contrasts with paper surveys, which can be inconvenient and time-consuming for respondents.

Another advantage of digital surveys is that they are often quicker and easier to complete than paper surveys. Because they can be filled out electronically, digital surveys often have fewer questions and take less time to complete, which can make them more appealing to respondents. This is particularly important in situations where the surveyor is trying to gather feedback from many people, as it can be more efficient to use a digital survey rather than a paper survey.

Digital surveys also offer several other benefits over paper surveys. As a Marine Corps Recruiter you can keep using the same Google Form for the entirety of your time on recruiting duty. This will allow you to have access to all people whom you have ever given a class talk at any time. Finally, digital surveys are often more accurate and reliable than paper surveys, as they can be designed to eliminate errors or inconsistencies that may occur when people fill out paper surveys by hand.

Overall, digital surveys are more valuable than paper surveys in a variety of ways. From their convenience and efficiency to time-saving benefits, digital surveys offer many advantages over their paper counterparts, making them a valuable tool for recruiters looking to gather data.

Having Friends in The Right Places

Anecdote – A Recruiter and a School Board

A recruiter named Jack was having issues with a hostile principal who just did not like the military, so he decided to attend a local school board meeting.

The school board meeting was a typical one, with discussions about budget cuts, new policies, and progress reports from various committees. The members of the board sat around a long table, with the superintendent at the head, while various teachers, parents, and community members watched from the audience.

As the meeting dragged on, the Marine Corps recruiter sat quietly in the back of the room, observing with interest. He was a tall, imposing figure in his crisp uniform, and his presence had not gone unnoticed by the board members.

When the meeting finally came to an end, the recruiter made his way to the front of the room and approached one of the board members, a middle-aged man named Tom.

"Excuse me, sir," the recruiter said, extending his hand. "My name is Staff Sergeant Jack Thompson. I just wanted to introduce myself and see if you'd be interested in getting some coffee with me."

Tom hesitated for a moment, caught off guard by the unexpected invitation. But something about the recruiter's friendly demeanor put him at ease, and he found himself saying yes.

The two men made their way to a nearby coffee shop and sat down at a small table. Tom expected the recruiter to start talking about enlistment and the benefits of joining the Marine Corps for high school students, but to his surprise, Jack simply listened as Tom talked about his job as a school board member and the various challenges he faced.

As they talked, Tom found himself opening up to Jack in a way he hadn't to anyone else in a long time. They began to sit down for coffee quite often and eventually Jack mentioned to Tom his frustration with some of the school's administrators, including one particularly rude principal who had given Jack a hard time when he visited the school to talk to students about military careers.

A week later, the recruiter, Jack, received a phone call from the same principal, asking if they could meet to discuss ways to improve relations between the school and the military. The recruiter agreed to the meeting, and when he arrived, he found the principal to be much more friendly and receptive than he had been in the past.

Tom and Jack continued to meet for coffee and discuss various topics facing the school district. Through their conversations, Tom began to see the value of the Marine Corps and the role it played in shaping young people's lives. And as for the once-hostile principal, he became one of the recruiter's biggest supporters, inviting him to speak at school events and even joining him for coffee on occasion.

Thanks to their unlikely friendship, both Tom and Jack were able to make a positive impact on the school and its students, and they remained close friends for many years to come.

Reflection

You see, if the recruiter had begged the principal to allow him greater access to the school, he would have likely received less access and lost the principal's respect. However, by building a relationship with someone who held power over the principal, the recruiter was able to influence the principal and gain the same level of access to the high school as any college, as required by law.

This story, while fiction, shows that you should cultivate relationships with individuals and organizations in your community that have a stake in the local high schools. This includes the school board, parent-teacher association, and teacher's union. By establishing yourself as a known and respected member of the community, you will be in a better position to gain access to the schools and connect with potential recruits. It is essential to be an active and involved member of the community, rather than an outsider.

By building trust and gaining the respect of others, you will be able to fulfill your role more effectively as a recruiter and make a positive impact on the lives of young people in your area. So, it is crucial to take the time to develop relationships with key individuals and groups in your community, as you never know when they may be able to assist you in gaining access or provide valuable insights and connections.

Good Tips on High Schools

1. Hanging QR Codes – Hang a Poster with a QR Code Leading to the ePPC Portal in every classroom. This is a good passive way to generate ePPCs.

2. Take Photographs of Sign-Up Rosters – High Schools typically have sign-up rosters for various activities. If you see one of these, take a picture of it and use the data contained to update your lists.

3. Volunteer to serve as a chaperone – High School Dances often need chaperones to make sure everything stays safe. Offering to be a chaperone allows you a good opportunity to be present at the school and to build rapport with the teachers, parents, and other staff members who are also there on chaperone duty.

4. Make every effort to get the ASVAB: Career Exploration Program into your schools. This will generate leads for all the branches, but you want to be the one to set it up. It gives you another chance to get in front of the staff and you can volunteer to monitor the test. During the test a roster is generated for all who showed up, the students who voluntarily showed up are usually good prospects. Additionally, if you have any students who cannot pass the test, have them take it at the high school. It may be anecdotal, but I have a much higher passing rate on the high school paper test compared to the electronic one at MEPS.

5. Leave a letter inviting teachers to the Educator's Workshop in each of their school mailboxes. Every school has mailboxes for the teachers, this is a perfect place to leave a letter about the Educator's workshop and any other information you deem valuable. Don't

overdo it though, you do not want to look like spam.

6. Do not purchase an Ad in the high school yearbook, in my opinion, it is not a cost-effective use of your funds.

7. Ask the school newspaper to do a story on you and any command recruiters who come back to visit.

8. Ask for a list of military veterans on the school staff. These people will be more receptive to class talks and can be powerful allies within the school.□

4 THE GROUND GAME

Chapter Introduction

As I look back on my three years on recruiting duty, I can't help but think about the words of Carb, an 8412 Career Recruiter whom I met during my PAR training in February of 2018. He told me that by the time a recruiter is nearing the end of their tour, they should be able to run for mayor in their area of operations and win. At the time, I remember thinking how crazy and hyperbolic that sounded, but as I reflect on my experiences as a recruiter, I realize just how much truth there is to Carb's words.

One of the key components I believe is essential in being a successful recruiter is going "house to house" and "street to street" in your area of operations (AO). This means actively seeking out potential recruits, rather than waiting for them to come to you. It's a proactive approach that requires a lot of hard work and dedication, but it's also an incredibly effective way to find prospects.

The idea behind going house to house and street to street is getting a physical message from you to every single senior at your priority high schools, early in the school year, whether by mail or by dropping it off in person. If you work in a small enough town, it may even mean getting a letter to every single house in the whole town. This may seem like a daunting task, but it's essential for reaching as many potential recruits as possible.

To make this approach successful, it's important to have the support of the Recruiting Station. Make them work for you. There is an idea of the "rule of seven" in Marketing. This rule states that a prospect needs to "hear" the advertiser's message at least seven times before they'll take action to buy that product or service. You should ask for financial support from your Command for things like postage and business cards, as well as support from ComStrat Marine in the form of signs and other promotional materials. The idea is to flood your AO with information about how to contact you, forever working towards the "Marketing Rule of Seven" with every prospect on your list.

I strongly feel, going house to house and street to street is invaluable in finding the best recruits. It allows you to build relationships with potential prospects and their families, and it gives you an opportunity to answer any questions or concerns they may have about joining the Marines. It's also a great way to get your message to the community and understand their needs and values, which can be incredibly helpful when it comes to recruiting.

In the next few chapters, we'll delve deeper into improving your "ground game" and getting your message out physically in your community. We'll discuss how to map out the most effective routes, how to effectively use Command Recruiters, and how you can create your own "direct mail" program. The intent is for you to finish this part of the book clearly understanding how to make yourself known in your AO and effectively reach out to potential recruits.

House to House, Street to Street

Anecdote – The Battle of Hue City

The Battle of Hue City was a defining moment in the Vietnam War, and it was a brutal, house-to-house and street-to-street fight that tested the mettle of the United States Marines who were called upon to retake the city from the North Vietnamese Army (NVA) and the Viet Cong (VC).

The city of Hue was a cultural and historical hub in Vietnam, and it was also strategically important as it sat on the main highway that connected the north and south of the country. So, when the NVA and VC launched a surprise attack on Hue during the Tet Offensive in January 1968, the United States Marines were among the first to respond.

The fighting was intense and fierce from the start, with the NVA and VC using their knowledge of the narrow streets and dense urban environment to their advantage. The United States Marines were forced to fight house-to-house and street-to-street, using their superior training and firepower to slowly push the enemy out of the city.

The United States Marines faced numerous challenges as they fought to clear the city. The narrow streets and densely packed buildings made it difficult for them to use their heavier weapons and armor, forcing them to rely on their training and tactics to overcome the enemy. The NVA and VC were also well-entrenched in the city, and they had the advantage of fighting on familiar ground.

Despite these challenges, the United States Marines were relentless in their efforts to retake the city. They faced heavy resistance at every turn, with the NVA and VC putting up a fierce fight to hold onto their positions. One of the most iconic moments of the Battle of Hue City was the Siege of the Citadel, where a small group of United States Marines and South Vietnamese soldiers held off a much larger NVA force. The Citadel was a fortress located in the center of the city, and it was a crucial strategic location. Despite being vastly outnumbered, the United States Marines and South Vietnamese soldiers held their ground, fighting off wave after wave of attackers.

Finally, after more than a month of grueling combat, the United States Marines and their South Vietnamese allies were able to push the NVA and VC out of the city. The victory came at a high cost, with both sides suffering heavy casualties.

The Battle of Hue City was a turning point in the Vietnam War, and it was a testament to the bravery and determination of the United States Marines who fought there. It was also a major propaganda victory for the North Vietnamese, as they were able to show that they could hold their own against the highly trained and well-equipped United States Marines in a major city. The city of Hue was left in ruins after the battle, with many of the buildings damaged or destroyed by the fighting. The United States Marines worked tirelessly to rebuild the city and restore order, going through every neighborhood to clear the remaining enemy forces and secure the city.

The city of Hue eventually began to rebuild and recover. The United States Marines played a crucial role in this process, working alongside the South Vietnamese people to rebuild the city and restore hope for the future. Today, the city of Hue has been restored and has become a popular tourist destination in Vietnam. Visitors can still see the scars of the war, with many of the buildings bearing the marks of the fierce fighting that took place there. But despite its violent past, Hue is now a thriving and vibrant city, a testament to the resilience and determination of its people and the United States Marines who fought to defend it. The bravery and sacrifice of the United States Marines will always be remembered by the people of Hue and the wider Vietnam War community.

In the aftermath of the Battle of Hue City, the United States Marines were hailed as heroes for their bravery and determination in the face of overwhelming odds. They had fought against a formidable enemy, and they had come out on top, defending the city and the people of Hue from the threat of the NVA and VC.

Despite the heavy losses suffered by both sides, the Battle of Hue City was ultimately a victory for the United States Marines and their

South Vietnamese allies. It was a turning point in the Vietnam War, and it demonstrated the resilience and determination of the South Vietnamese people and the United States Marines who fought to defend them.

□

Reflection

Using the battle of Hue City as inspiration, it's clear that going house-to-house and street-to-street can be an effective strategy for reaching potential recruits and achieving the desired outcome. This approach involves personally visiting the homes of potential recruits, building relationships, and establishing a personal connection with them.

As a canvassing recruiter, it's important to make sure that you have covered every sector in your area of operation and reached out to every potential recruit. One effective way to do this is by going house-to-house and street-to-street, conducting home visits, and personally engaging with potential recruits. Home visits are underutilized because nobody has been taught how to make them effective. Driving 40 minutes round trip to knock on one door makes no sense logistically. But, if you were able to hit 20 houses in that trip, the value of the drive increases exponentially.

Mapping software like Google Earth can be especially valuable in this process. By plotting every single person on your current senior list, recent graduate list, and 11th-grade list on Google Earth, you can create effective routes to conduct a home visit on every single prospect on your lists. This allows you to efficiently cover all areas of your recruiting territory and ensure that you have reached out to every prospect.

Conducting Home Visits like this can be time-consuming and labor-intensive, but it can also be highly effective in reaching potential recruits who may not have otherwise been engaged through other means.

In addition to visiting homes, you can also use the mapping software to plot schools, community centers, and other locations where potential recruits may be found. This can help you to reach a wider pool of potential recruits and ensure that you are covering all areas of your recruiting territory. For more information on how to effectively use mapping software, please refer to Chapter 2 of this book where I go into detail on the subject.

Your Own Direct Mail Program

Anecdote One – Personal Observations of the Official Direct Mail Program

As I was conducting my time on recruiting duty, I noticed that none of the students I spoke with had received any direct mail. This piqued my curiosity because I believe that direct mail would be an effective means of communication. From a logical perspective, I tried to consider the perspective of a high school student. They may not receive many letters, so a letter addressed specifically to them could stand out. Therefore, I began to investigate the reason for this lack of direct mail.

Upon speaking with individuals from Headquarters Marine Corps and several 8412s, I was informed that the distribution of direct mail is based on the "propensity for enlistment" in certain areas. Essentially, if a region has a lower tendency for enlistment (such as the San Francisco Bay Area), it will receive fewer direct mail pieces compared to an area with a higher tendency for enlistment (like San Antonio). This is how the advertising company Wunderman Thompson (previously known as J Walter Thompson) conducts its business for the Marines.

While we could simply complain about the unequal distribution of direct mail, I believe it would be more productive to act. But first, let's look to the past for examples of the benefits of using direct mail as a means of communication.

Anecdote Two – Direct Mail in United States Elections

Political direct mail has long been a crucial element of political marketing strategies, but few campaigns have received as much attention as those during the 2008 and 2016 elections. During these elections, multichannel marketing played a central role in the political arena, with both President Obama in 2008 and President Trump in 2016 effectively leveraging the power of digital platforms such as websites, blogs, and social media to reach and mobilize voters. Both campaigns received significant recognition for their use of these platforms.

However, it is worth noting that the success of these campaigns was not solely due to their digital efforts. Both Obama and Trump also invested significant resources in their direct mail campaigns, which played a crucial role in reaching and mobilizing voters. While the specifics of these campaigns may vary, it is clear that both presidents understood the power of direct mail as a means of reaching and engaging with voters.

During his campaign, President Obama's team excelled in the use of direct mail, creating effective and visually stunning pieces that resonated with voters. They developed a clear and consistent message that reflected Obama's approach and values and conveyed this message in a direct and straightforward manner.

To further enhance the impact of their direct mail campaigns, Obama's team made full use of outside envelope (OE) messaging and imaging. The outside envelope is the outermost envelope that contains the direct mail piece, and it is typically addressed to the recipient and includes a postage stamp or indicia. It is an important element of a direct mail campaign because it is the first thing the recipient sees when they receive the mail, and therefore it is essential to consider its design and messaging to create a strong first impression and encourage the recipient to open the mail.

To this end, Obama's team used eye-catching graphics and images, clear and concise calls-to-action, and personalized elements such as the recipient's name or location to design their outside envelopes. These techniques helped to enhance the visual appeal of their direct mail pieces and grab the attention of voters. Obama's team also carefully considered the language used in their direct mail campaigns and tailored it to the target audience. This helped to create a sense of connection and resonance with voters and contributed to the overall effectiveness of the campaign. By utilizing the power of direct mail in these ways, Obama's team was able to reach and mobilize voters in a compelling and impactful manner.

The 2016 presidential election between Donald Trump and Hillary Clinton was a closely contested race, with both candidates using a variety of strategies to reach and mobilize voters. One aspect of their campaigns that has garnered attention is their use of direct mail. According to Federal Election Commission (FEC) filings, Trump spent 37 cents of every campaign dollar on direct mail, while Clinton spent 20 cents. Despite being outspent on direct mail by Clinton, Trump ultimately emerged victorious in the election.

"I'm a very cost-effective politician." - President Trump

Despite having a reputation for being fiscally mindful, President Trump's direct mail campaign was no exception. His campaign invested a total of $29 million in printing and postage for its direct mail efforts, but how did this relatively frugal campaign contribute to his success? One key factor was Trump's targeting of rural voters, a significant portion of his base. By purchasing lists of rural voters and focusing his direct mail efforts on this group, Trump was able to effectively mobilize and encourage turnout among this demographic.

This strategic targeting, combined with Trump's cost-effective approach, helped to make his direct mail campaign a success.

In the 2016 presidential election, President Trump's use of direct mail allowed him to reach voters in a more unobtrusive way compared to other methods such as television ads and social media commercials. While his opponent, Hillary Clinton, spent significantly more on TV ads ($140 million) compared to Trump ($40 million), many voters became tired of being inundated with political commercials and tuned them out. In contrast, direct mail allowed the recipients to view and engage with the material on their own time, making it a more appealing and effective medium for political campaigns.

This is especially true for younger generations like millennials, who may be more likely to respond to tangible objects like direct mail. In fact, according to a study conducted by the Data & Marketing Association, direct mail has a higher response rate among younger generations compared to other marketing channels. This suggests that campaigns that utilize direct mail may be more effective at reaching and mobilizing younger voters.

Reflection

It is important to consider every possible avenue for reaching and engaging with potential recruits, and one effective method is using your own direct mail. Whether you are recruiting in an area with a high propensity for enlistment or not, it can be beneficial to write a letter introducing yourself to the students on your list.

To make the most impact, it is recommended that the letter be in Naval Letter Format and look as official as possible. You can ask for support from your Recruiting Station (RS) to provide envelopes and cover the cost of postage. If you are particularly keen on this approach, you can also have your Senior Non-Commissioned Officer in Charge (SNCOIC) include a request for logistical support in their mission restatement letter. Putting this in writing can help to ensure that your request is considered and can potentially increase the chances of it being approved.

Of course, ultimately the decision on whether to fund this endeavor will fall on your commanding officer, who has the final say in the matter. If they do not approve the funding, you may choose to fund the project yourself, as investing in your recruiting efforts can be a valuable investment in your future and the time you are able to spend with your family.

Once you have the necessary resources, you can use Microsoft Word's "Mail Merge" feature to print each student's name and address on the letters. After packing the letters into envelopes, the only thing left to do is to mail them out. This can be an excellent task for Command Recruiters to take on, and the inspiration for this idea came from the legendary Carb. He was the wizard at making effective use of your Command Recruiters, a chapter we will cover next.

As we have seen from the examples of the Obama and Trump campaigns, direct mail can be a highly effective tool for reaching and engaging with prospects. It allows you to target specific demographics and reach them in a more unobtrusive way compared to other methods such as television ads and social media. Direct mail also allows recipients to view and engage with the material on their own time, making it an appealing and effective medium for recruiters, especially considering younger generations like millennials may be more responsive to tangible objects.

Using Command Recruiters

Anecdote – The Ballad of the Recruiter's Assistant

Private First Class (PFC) John Shmuckatelli was a young Marine who had recently graduated from recruit training and was excited to return home to support his local recruiting station as a Command Recruiter. He had completed communications school at 29 Palms, California, and was eager to see his family and friends and make a difference in his community.

As PFC Shmuckatelli arrived at the recruiting station, he was greeted by his recruiter, Staff Sergeant Smith. However, things quickly took a turn for the worse as Staff Sergeant Smith noticed that PFC Shmuckatelli was not wearing his dress blue bravos. PFC Shmuckatelli explained that he had not been told to bring the uniform, but Staff Sergeant Smith was clearly annoyed by this and rudely told him that he should have shown initiative and brought the correct uniform.

PFC Shmuckatelli was embarrassed and disappointed by this

exchange, feeling like he had let down his recruiter and the Marine Corps. He had always been proud of his uniform and wanted to present himself in the best possible way, and now he felt like he had failed in this regard.

As Staff Sergeant Smith handed him a stack of blank forms, PFC Shmuckatelli felt a sense of dread wash over him. He was told that he needed to get 10 forms filled out before he could go home, and that he needed to do this every day for the 20 days he was on Recruiter's Assistance duty. PFC Shmuckatelli knew that this was going to be a long and grueling process, and he couldn't help but wonder when he would finally be able to spend time with his family.

The days dragged on as PFC Shmuckatelli worked diligently to fill out the forms, feeling frustrated and disheartened by the lack of progress he seemed to be making. He had always been a hard worker and was not opposed to putting in long hours, but this assignment seemed to offer little in the way of reward or fulfillment. He had no idea how his efforts were contributing to the overall mission, and he felt like he was just going through the motions without any real purpose or direction.

As the days passed, PFC Shmuckatelli began to feel increasingly agitated and longing for the comfort and familiarity of a barracks room. At least there he felt like he was useful. He spent little time with his family and friends, and he felt like he was wasting time. He also found himself feeling resentful of Staff Sergeant Smith and the other recruiters, who seemed to have no understanding or appreciation of the sacrifices he was making.

Despite these challenges, PFC Shmuckatelli remained determined to complete his assignment and fulfill his duties to the best of his ability. He knew that he had a responsibility to the Marine Corps and to his country, and he was determined to do his part.

Finally, after what seemed like an eternity, PFC Shmuckatelli's 20 days on Recruiter's Assistance duty came to an end. He was relieved and overjoyed to be returning to his barracks room, and he couldn't wait to see his friends and finally get some much-needed rest and relaxation.

As he left the recruiting station for the last time, PFC Shmuckatelli was happy to finally be done with recruiter's assistance. The Staff Sergeant didn't thank him for his work and told him to try and come back again in a few months. But if there was one thing that PFC Shmuckatelli had learned during his time on Recruiter's Assistance duty, it was that no matter what, next time he would just use his annual leave days. He had learned the hard way that the sacrifices and inconveniences of Recruiter's Assistance were simply not worth it, and he vowed to never put himself through that again. From now on, he would use his annual leave days to take time off and enjoy the comfort and familiarity of home.

Reflection

Depressing right? Unfortunately, that story is how a lot of Marines I have talked to in the fleet tell me what their time on recruiter's assistance was like. It's unfortunate because you really do need

Command Recruiters to get the job done on recruiting duty effectively and efficiently.

Command Recruiters allow you to execute a successful ground game in the recruitment process. The Sergeant Major plays a crucial role in the success of the Command Recruiting Program, and it is important to constantly seek out and request the presence of Command Recruiters. If necessary, reach out to the Sergeant Major and advocate for Marines who are being told they are unable to return due to conflicting duties. Remember, recruiting is a vital mission for the Marine Corps and should be prioritized above everything besides direct conflict. If a Marine is not currently deployed or deploying in the next few months, there is no reason they should not be able to return and assist with recruitment efforts.

But if you want Command Recruiters, they must be given something meaningful to do while they are there. One way to ensure that Command Recruiters are given meaningful tasks and remain happy during their time at the recruiting station is to provide clear communication and expectations from the beginning. Before they even leave their schoolhouse or duty station to come to the recruiting station, it is important to inform them about what uniforms they need to bring, the hours they can expect to be in the office, and the duties they will be expected to complete. By clearly communicating these expectations, Command Recruiters will know exactly what is expected of them and can focus on completing the tasks at hand. Also, respect their time.

If you have them coming at 8am to pack letters, make sure you are there before them. Have coffee and snacks ready for them to eat. Have all the materials out for them to use. And let them know exactly how much they need to get done. Telling them to keep going forever is not fair to them, they deserve to be informed about what tasks they are being asked to complete. If you are going to have them write letters to their former teachers, have an example of what you need it to look like, have a list of all the faculty at their former high school, and leave them until the letters are done.

Another way to keep Command Recruiters happy is to make sure they have a sense of purpose and accomplishment. Providing them with clear goals and tasks and setting aside dedicated time for them to complete these tasks, will help them feel productive and valued. Additionally, it is important to show appreciation for their contributions and to thank them for their efforts. This can be as simple as providing refreshments or snacks during their time at the recruiting station or expressing genuine gratitude for their efforts. You can never thank a CDR too many times and allow them the freedom to use their skills and expertise to contribute to the recruiting mission in meaningful ways.

CDRs will do two things, what you ask them to do and what you let them do. They usually do not need to be micro-managed. If you do not have anything for them, do not waste their time. Let them spend time with their family. Finally, you can never thank a CDR too many times.□

□

Hearts and Minds

Anecdote – The Iraq War

The Hearts and Minds campaign in Iraq, implemented by General James Mattis in 2003, was a groundbreaking approach to counterinsurgency warfare. Rather than simply relying on brute force and military might, General Mattis recognized the importance of winning over the hearts and minds of the Iraqi people. He knew that to truly defeat the insurgency, he would need to address the root causes of the conflict and build relationships with the local population.

General Mattis began by working closely with tribal leaders and community leaders, trying to understand their needs and concerns. He also worked to restore basic services such as electricity and clean water to the people of Iraq, knowing that these were essential for building trust and support.

Despite facing significant challenges and setbacks, General Mattis was determined to succeed in his mission. As he famously said, "I come in peace. I didn't bring artillery. But I'm pleading with you, with tears in his eyes: If you f--- with me, I'll kill you all." This quote, while perhaps controversial, speaks to General Mattis' commitment to winning over the hearts and minds of the Iraqi people and his willingness to do whatever it takes to achieve his goals. His desire to build a relationship with the Iraqi people and treat them with respect was captured most brilliantly in a letter he wrote to 1st Marine Division in March 2003, the full text of the letter is below:

General Mattis Letter to 1st Marine Division

"For decades, Saddam Hussein has tortured, imprisoned, raped, and murdered the Iraqi people; invaded neighboring countries without provocation; and threatened the world with weapons of mass destruction. The time has come to end his reign of terror. On your young shoulders rest the hopes of mankind.

When I give you the word, together we will cross the Line of Departure, close with those forces that choose to fight, and destroy them. Our fight is not with the Iraqi people, nor is it with members of the Iraqi Army who choose to surrender. While we will move swiftly and aggressively against those who resist, we will treat all others with decency, demonstrating chivalry and soldierly compassion for people who have endured a lifetime under Saddam's oppression.

Chemical attacks, treachery, and the use of the innocent as human shields can be expected, as can unethical tactics. Take it all in stride. Be the hunter, not the hunted: never allow your unit to be caught with its guard down. Use good judgment and act in the best interest of our Nation.

You are part of the world's most feared and trusted force. Engage your brain before you engage your weapon. Share your courage with each other as we enter the uncertain terrain north of the Line of

Departure. Keep faith with your comrades on your left and right and Marine Air overhead. Fight with a happy heart and strong spirit.

For the mission's sake, our country's sake, and the sake of the men who carried the Division's colors in past battles -- who fought for life and never lost their nerve -- carry out your mission and keep your honor clean. Demonstrate to the world that there is "No Better Friend, No Worse Enemy" than a U.S. Marine."

J.N Mattis

Major General, U.S. Marines

Commanding

General Mattis' Hearts and Minds campaign in Iraq was a prime example of the Marine Corps' commitment to building positive relationships with the local population. As the commanding officer of the 1st Marine Division, General Mattis recognized the importance of winning the trust and support of the Iraqi people to achieve long-term stability and success in the region.

To achieve this, General Mattis implemented several innovative initiatives designed to engage with the local population and address their needs and concerns. One of the key components of this campaign was the establishment of community liaison teams, which were tasked with building relationships with local leaders and working to address their needs and concerns.

Another key aspect of the Hearts and Minds campaign was the emphasis on building trust and respect through dialogue and collaboration. General Mattis understood that to effectively address the challenges facing the region, it was necessary to work closely with local leaders and build a sense of mutual understanding and respect.

One of the most memorable quotes from General Mattis in this regard came during a press conference in 2005 when he said: "I don't care how many bullets I have. It doesn't mean a damn thing if I can't get the Iraqi people to believe that I'm here to help them."

Throughout the Hearts and Minds campaign, General Mattis and his team worked tirelessly to build positive relationships with the Iraqi people. Whether it was through providing humanitarian aid and assistance or working to improve infrastructure and provide essential services, the Marines were dedicated to building a brighter future for the people of Iraq.

In the end, the Hearts and Minds campaign remains a shining example of the Marine Corps' commitment to building positive relationships with the local population and working to achieve long-term stability and success in challenging environments. Despite the many challenges and setbacks that were encountered along the way, the Marines never wavered in their commitment to the people of Iraq, and their efforts played a crucial role in helping to pave the way for a brighter and more prosperous future.

Reflection

The spirit of the "hearts and minds" campaign in Iraq, which was implemented by General James Mattis during the early years of the Iraq War, can be applied to building relationships with communities on Marine Corps Recruiting duty in several ways. At its core, the "hearts and minds" campaign was focused on building trust and understanding between the United States military and the Iraqi people, in order to promote stability and peace in the region. This same approach can be applied to building relationships with communities on recruiting duty, as it involves actively engaging with and listening to the needs and concerns of local residents, and working to build a sense of trust and respect.

One key aspect of the "hearts and minds" campaign was the importance of building relationships with local leaders and community members. General Mattis and his team worked closely with tribal leaders, religious leaders, and other influential figures in the Iraqi community to gain their support and cooperation. On recruiting duty, SNCOICs and recruiters can adopt a similar approach by building relationships with local leaders and community members in their assigned area. This could involve attending community meetings, participating in local events and festivals, and simply trying to get to know people and understand their perspectives. By building relationships with local leaders and community members, recruiters can better understand the needs and concerns of their community, and work to address them in a way that fosters trust and mutual understanding.

Another important aspect of the "hearts and minds" campaign

was the focus on transparency and honesty. General Mattis and his team made a concerted effort to be transparent and upfront with the Iraqi people about their intentions and actions. They were open about their goals and objectives, and made an effort to listen to the concerns and feedback of local residents. On recruiting duty, SNCOICs and recruiters can adopt a similar approach by being open and transparent with their community. This could involve being upfront about their goals and objectives, and actively seeking out feedback and input from local residents. By being transparent and honest, recruiters can build trust and respect with their community, and work to create a positive and collaborative relationship.

Finally, the "hearts and minds" campaign in Iraq was focused on building lasting and sustainable relationships with the Iraqi people. General Mattis and his team worked to create long-term partnerships with local communities and to support the development of local infrastructure and institutions. On recruiting duty, SNCOICs and recruiters can adopt a similar approach by building long-term relationships with their community, and working to support local development and growth. This could involve working with local schools and institutions to provide resources and support, or collaborating with community organizations to address local needs and challenges. By building lasting and sustainable relationships with their community, recruiters can create a strong foundation for future collaboration and cooperation.

Overall, the spirit of the "hearts and minds" campaign in Iraq can be applied to building relationships with communities on recruiting duty by focusing on building relationships with local leaders and community members, being transparent and honest, and building lasting and sustainable partnerships. By adopting these approaches, recruiters can create strong and positive relationships with their community, and work to promote stability and understanding. As General Mattis once said, "The most important six inches on the battlefield is between your ears. Success is a matter of will and understanding – the will to do what must be done and the understanding of what it takes to do it." By applying this mindset to their work on recruiting duty, SNCOICs and recruiters can create positive and lasting relationships with their community, and work to promote understanding and cooperation.

5 RECRUITING IS A TEAM SPORT

Chapter Introduction

This is the shortest chapter introduction of the whole book because I want it to stick. No matter how skilled an individual recruiter may be, they cannot succeed without a strong team supporting them. It is crucial to prioritize building and maintaining strong relationships with within your team,, as these connections have lasting effects even after one's time in this role comes to an end. Remember to always prioritize the needs of the team and avoid selfish behavior.

The First Rule of Leading a Team

Anecdote – Leading Like Trancoley

I began my role as the Staff Non-Commissioned Officer in

Charge (SNCOIC) for Recruiting Sub-Station Fairfield in November 2018, just eight months after I had been working as a production recruiter. My Commanding Officer, Major Clinton K. Hall, approached me in the Recruiting Station Headquarters the day before the Marine Corps Birthday and asked if I was ready to take on the position in Fairfield. From that day forward, the office was mine. Despite my confidence and recent success as a top-performing recruiter, I quickly learned that leading a team required more than just setting goals and holding people accountable.

My first experience as a SNCOIC was rocky, as I struggled to build relationships and earn the respect of my team. One recruiter and I nearly came to blows, and another recruiter, openly admitted that he did not respect me. I was trying to do what I thought was right, but I was not a part of the team.

It was through the guidance of Thomas McKenzie, the former SNCOIC who was now serving as an assistant recruiter instructor, that I began to understand the importance of being a part of the team. McKenzie frequently checked in on his former team and provided support and guidance. However, it was my assistant SNCOIC, Jevon Trancoley, who truly exemplified what it meant to be a leader.

Jevon Trancoley was a crucial member of the team and an invaluable source of guidance and support for me as the SNCOIC. He was always willing to go beyond to ensure that the team was working cohesively and effectively. Trancoley was deeply invested in the development and training of those he worked with, and he made a genuine effort to get to know each member of the team on a personal level. He never placed himself above anybody and he was always approachable and willing to listen. He was adept at diffusing conflicts and maintaining a positive work environment. Trancoley was also a skilled leader in terms of setting and achieving goals. He was able to clearly articulate his expectations and hold team members accountable, while also providing the necessary support and resources to ensure their success.

It was through Trancoley that I learned an important lesson about being a leader: "The first rule of leading a team is to be a part of the team."

Reflection

Building a good team, that you are a part of, is a crucial aspect of leadership, as it allows individuals to work together towards a common goal and achieve success. To build a good team, it is important to focus on building relationships, setting clear goals and expectations, and providing support and resources.

Building a good team is about the establishment of strong relationships. According to General Mattis, "I could command in 15 minutes a day, the rest of his time was coaching." This quote highlights the importance of building relationships with team members and providing ongoing support and guidance. By taking the time to get to know each member of the team on a personal level, leaders can create a sense of community and foster a positive work environment. This can involve activities such as team-building exercises, regular one-on-one meetings, and creating opportunities for open communication and feedback.

It is also important for leaders to set clear goals and expectations for the team. This involves establishing a vision for the team and communicating this vision effectively. Leaders should also break down larger goals into smaller, more attainable objectives, and provide the necessary resources and support to help team members achieve these objectives. Setting goals and expectations not only helps to keep the team focused and motivated, but it also allows for better tracking of progress and the identification of areas for improvement.

Finally, providing support and resources to team members is a crucial aspect of building a good team. This can include training and development opportunities, as well as access to the necessary tools and resources to complete tasks. Leaders should also be willing to listen to the needs and concerns of team members and provide guidance and support as needed. By providing support and resources, leaders can help make sure team members are able to perform at their best and contribute to the overall success of the team.

By taking the time to coach and support team members, leaders can create a cohesive and effective team that is able to achieve success.

Humility, The 15th Leadership Trait

Anecdote – George Washington and Humility

George Washington was a man of remarkable humility and selflessness, qualities that were on full display when he made the decision to only serve two terms as President of the United States.

At the time of Washington's presidency, there was little doubt about who would be the nation's first leader. His strong leadership during the Revolutionary War had earned him the respect and admiration of the American people, and he was widely seen as the most qualified candidate for the job. However, Washington was not motivated by personal ambition or a desire for power. He largely detested politics, and he particularly despised the growing factions and political parties that were beginning to emerge in the fledgling nation.

Despite the many challenges and responsibilities of the presidency, Washington remained true to his principles and his commitment to the greater good. In 1796, after serving just two terms, he stepped aside and made way for a new president.

The impact of Washington's decision was far-reaching and enduring. By choosing to only serve two terms, Washington set a precedent that would shape the course of American history for centuries to come. His actions demonstrated the importance of the peaceful transition of power and the rule of law, and they set the stage for a system of government that is based on the idea of a balance of power and the separation of branches.

Today, the tradition of limiting presidents to two terms is codified in law, but it was Washington's humility and selflessness that made it possible. His legacy serves as a reminder of the importance of putting the needs of the nation above our own personal interests, and it inspires us to strive for a government that is responsive, accountable, and dedicated to the common good.

Anecdote – Socrates and Humility

Socratic humility was an important aspect of the philosopher's worldview and had significant implications for how he approached life and learning. To Socrates, humility was not a sign of weakness, but rather a recognition of the limits of human understanding and the importance of seeking knowledge from others.

In his famous "Apology," Socrates famously declared, "I am the wisest man alive, for I know one thing, and that is that I know nothing." This statement might seem paradoxical at first glance, but it demonstrates Socrates' humility and his recognition that human understanding is limited. By acknowledging that he knew nothing, Socrates was able to open himself up to learning and seeking knowledge from others.

Socratic humility also involved a willingness to question and challenge one's own assumptions and beliefs. In Plato's "Theaetetus," Socrates says, "The unexamined life is not worth living." This statement suggests that pursuing wisdom and understanding requires a willingness to question and challenge one's beliefs and assumptions. By embracing this attitude, individuals can cultivate humility and work towards a greater understanding of the world around them.

In addition to acknowledging one's limitations and seeking knowledge from others, Socratic humility also involved an openness to learning from those who might disagree with one's beliefs. Socratic humility was a fundamental aspect of the philosopher's worldview and had significant implications for how he approached life and learning.

Anecdote – Marcus Aurelius on Humility

Marcus Aurelius, the Roman philosopher, and Emperor had a deep conviction in the significance of humility. He believed that humility was a crucial virtue that enabled individuals to live a fulfilling and meaningful life.

In "Meditations," Marcus writes, "It is not death that a man should fear, but he should fear never beginning to live." This statement suggests that Marcus saw fear as an obstacle that can prevent individuals from living a fulfilling life. By embracing humility and overcoming fear, individuals can live a life that is rich and meaningful.

To Marcus, humility was not about being self-effacing or lacking confidence, but rather about recognizing one's own limitations and the limitations of the world around us. In "Meditations," he writes, "It is not in the power of even the most skillful to find out the truth by his own ability, but he will find it by studying and questioning others." This statement suggests that Marcus believed that humility was crucial in the pursuit of knowledge and truth. By acknowledging one's own limitations and seeking guidance and knowledge from others, individuals can work towards a greater understanding of the world around them.

Marcus also believed that humility was essential in relationships with others. In "Meditations," he writes, "You should not be ashamed of your nature, because it is a nature that will be made perfect by the study of wisdom." This statement suggests that Marcus saw humility as allowing individuals to learn from others and to be open to learning and growing. By embracing humility, individuals can form stronger relationships with others and work towards mutual understanding and growth.

Marcus Aurelius had a strong belief in the importance of humility. He saw it as a virtue that enabled individuals to live fulfilling and meaningful lives, to seek knowledge and truth, and to form strong relationships with others.

Reflection

Humility is a crucial trait for any leader to possess, Marine Corps recruiting is no exception. It allows people to recognize their own limitations and limitations of their position and to put the needs of their team or organization above their own ego. Without humility, leaders may become overconfident or arrogant, leading to poor decision-making and a lack of respect from their followers.

One of the most prominent sources on the importance of

humility in a leader is the philosopher, Marcus Aurelius. In his famous work "Meditations," Aurelius writes, "The first rule is to keep an untroubled spirit. The second is to look things in the face and know them for what they are." This quote highlights the importance of humility in enabling a leader to remain level-headed and to see the world as it is, rather than through the distorted lens of ego. By keeping an open mind and being willing to listen to others, a humble leader is better equipped to make informed and well-reasoned decisions.

Another philosopher who emphasized the importance of humility was Socrates. In his famous dialogues, Socrates often challenged the assumptions of his fellow Athenians, encouraging them to question their beliefs and consider alternative perspectives. In one such dialogue, "The Apology," Socrates famously declared, "I am the wisest man alive, for I know one thing, and that is that I know nothing." This statement, which has become known as the "Socratic Paradox," illustrates the importance of humility in acknowledging our own limitations and seeking out knowledge and understanding.

In modern times, the importance of humility in leadership has been recognized by a variety of sources. For example, in a Harvard Business Review article on "Why Humility is the Most Important Quality of Leadership," the authors argue that humility is a key factor in creating a positive and productive work culture. They note that "humility is not about being meek or self-effacing; it's about having the confidence to admit when you don't know something and being open to learning from others." By demonstrating this type of humility, leaders can create an environment of trust and collaboration, which is essential for driving innovation and success.

Humility is a crucial trait for any leader to possess. By recognizing their own limitations and the limitations of their position, and by putting the needs of their team or organization above their own ego, leaders can demonstrate integrity and earn the respect of their followers. Whether it is Marcus Aurelius' emphasis on keeping an untroubled spirit or Socrates's acknowledgment of the Socratic Paradox, the importance of humility has been recognized by philosophers throughout history and continues to be recognized by modern sources as well.

Training

Anecdote – Honest Abe's Axe Applied to Recruiting

The quote "If I only had an hour to chop down a tree, I would spend the first 45 minutes sharpening his axe" by Abraham Lincoln is a powerful reminder of the importance of preparation and the value of investing time and effort into the tools and resources we use. When applied to the field of Recruiting, this quote highlights the importance of training and the role it plays in the success of Marine Corps Recruiters.

In the world of recruiting, success is often defined by the ability to close deals and bring in new contracts. However, simply being able to "chop down the tree," or close a contract, is not enough on its own. To be truly successful and thrive in the competitive market we are facing today, recruiters must be well-equipped and fully prepared to tackle the challenges they face. This is where training comes in.

Effective training in recruiting not only teaches recruiters the skills and knowledge they need to succeed, but it also helps to "sharpen their axe," or fine-tune their abilities and approach. This can include everything from learning about the enlistment options available to understanding the needs and motivations of prospects, to developing effective communication and negotiation skills. By investing in training and development, recruiters are better equipped to tackle the challenges they face and achieve success in their careers.

However, it is not just the initial training at the Basic Recruiter's Course that is important. Ongoing training and development are crucial for recruiters who want to stay sharp and continue to grow in their careers. The world of recruiting is constantly changing, and it is important for recruiters to stay up-to-date on the latest trends, techniques, and technologies in order to stay competitive. This can involve everything from holding weekly training with he SNCOIC to monthly training by the Recruiting Instructor. By continually "sharpening their axe," recruiters can keep their skills and knowledge relevant and effective, which can lead to greater success and career advancement. It must be taken seriously though by all parties to be effective.

In addition to the practical benefits of training and development, it is also important to consider the role of mindfulness and intentionality in the recruiting process. By taking the time to properly prepare and equip themselves through training, recruiters can approach their tasks with a greater sense of purpose and meaning. This mindfulness and intentionality can be seen in the way they interact with prospects, as they are able to truly understand and address their needs and concerns, rather than simply rushing to close a contract. This can lead to a more positive and rewarding recruiting experience for both the recruiting professional and the poolee, and it can foster long-term relationships and referrals.

The quote "If I only had an hour to chop down a tree, I would spend the first 45 minutes sharpening his axe" speaks to the importance of preparation and mindfulness in achieving success in the field of recruiting. By investing in training and development, recruiters are better equipped to tackle the challenges they face and achieve success in their careers. By approaching their tasks with intentionality and a focus on quality, they are able to create a more positive and rewarding recruiting experience for themselves and their customers. By continually "sharpening their axe," recruiters can stay competitive and continue to grow and advance in their careers.

Reflection

Recruiting is a difficult and often unenjoyable task for many people. Those who genuinely enjoy it are in the minority. It requires the ability to persuade others to do something they may not have otherwise considered, which can be mentally exhausting. Without proper training and practice, one is likely to fail at recruiting. To make sure that training is consistently occurring, it is advisable to set aside time every single week. For example, shutting down the office every Friday morning for training has proven to be effective in some cases. This can involve reviewing MC3, learning how to use social media more effectively, or practicing ways to engage potential recruits. In addition to this weekly training, it is important for leaders to continually coach and train their recruiters throughout the day.

Proper documentation of training is also essential. As Jeremy Shorten, my former Recruiter Instructor, once said, "you don't document the training just so you can pass a Systematic Recruiting Inspection. You do it so you have something to reference and look back on show you trained your guys to everything they need to know." This means that it is not only important to train, but also to have a record of it for future reference. By taking ownership of our recruiters' success, we can ensure that they are equipped with the necessary skills and knowledge to succeed.

And when it comes to the effectiveness of the recruiters, all burden falls on the shoulders of the SNCOIC. As Major Hall once pointed out to me, a leader's effectiveness should not be judged on their own personal achievements, but rather on the performance of their subordinates. If a leader is physically fit, but their team is struggling to meet fitness standards, it is a sign that they are not effectively leading and supporting their team. In the same spirit, if a SNCOIC says appears to be doing everything right himself but the results are not showing in his subordinates, it says a lot more about the SNCOIC than his recruiters.

It All Flows from Culture

Anecdote – A Shift in Culture

I had been working as the SNCOIC for the Recruiting Sub-Station in Fairfield for several months, but things were not going well. The office was struggling to meet its goals and morale was low. Despite this, Major Clinton K. Hall, my Commanding Officer, believed in me and decided to give me a second chance. He announced that the office in Fairfield would be splitting, with half of the recruiters moving to stand up a new office in American Canyon, California. I made the pitch to Major Hall about how to break down schools and recommended that my assistant SNCOIC become the SNCOIC of Fairfield while I took on the role in American Canyon. The Major agreed and we were split up, but he made it clear that I needed to perform in my new role.

I knew that I had to do something different in American Canyon to turn things around. I decided that the culture of the office would be different and that I would put everything into my recruiters. Whether we succeeded or failed, I wanted us to do it as a team. It wasn't easy at first and we had a few rough months, but eventually, things started to improve. By looking at our market share, I could see that we had more than 80% of the business, meaning that out of all the people joining the military in our area, 80% of them were joining the Marines and only 20% were going to other services. The team was happier and the Poolees (recruits who have completed the enlistment process but have not yet shipped to basic training) were shipped to recruit training at a steady rate. In fact, 100% of the young men and women we shipped graduated from recruit training during this time.

Looking back on my time in American Canyon, I know that the difference between my experiences in Fairfield and American Canyon was the culture. In American Canyon, I was a part of the team and we had a culture of winning as a team. We worked together and supported each other, and that made all the difference in our success. It was a valuable lesson for me and one that I carry with me to this day.

Reflection

In the world of Marine Corps Recruiting, "culture" refers to the values, beliefs, and behaviors that shape an organization and its members. It is a critical factor in the success or failure of a recruiting office, as it plays a significant role in determining how team members work together, communicate, and approach their tasks.

A positive and supportive culture can have several benefits for a recruiting team. It can foster a sense of collaboration and teamwork, which can lead to greater productivity and results. When team members feel valued and supported by their colleagues, they are more likely to feel motivated and engaged in their work. A positive culture, embodied by the idea of winning, can also create a sense of belonging and connection among team members, which can lead to greater job satisfaction and performance.

In addition to these internal benefits, a positive culture can also impact the way a recruiting team is perceived by external stakeholders, such as potential recruits and their families. When team members feel proud of their organization and its values, they are more likely to project a positive and professional image to others. This can be especially important in the field of Marine Corps Recruiting, where building trust and relationships with potential recruits is a key aspect of success.

On the other hand, a negative or toxic culture can have serious negative consequences for a recruiting team. It can lead to low morale, high RFC (relieved for cause) rates, and poor performance. When team members feel unsupported or mistreated, they are less likely to be engaged and motivated in their work, which can result in a decline in productivity and results. A toxic culture can also damage the reputation of an organization and impact its ability to attract and retain top talent.

So, how can leaders create and maintain a positive culture within their recruiting teams? There are a few strategies that can be effective. One is to establish clear values and expectations for team members and to consistently communicate and model these values in their own behavior. This can include things like honesty, transparency, and respect for others. It is also important to provide opportunities for team members to grow and develop and to recognize and reward their contributions. Another key factor is to foster open communication and encourage team members to share their ideas and feedback. This can be done through regular meetings and open-door policies, and by actively listening to and valuing the perspectives of team members.

Culture is an essential component of a successful recruiting team. A positive culture can foster collaboration, motivation, and engagement, and it can impact the way an organization is perceived by external stakeholders. On the other hand, a negative or toxic culture can lead to low morale, high turnover, and poor performance. Leaders can create and maintain a positive culture by establishing clear values, providing opportunities for growth and development, and fostering open communication. By prioritizing culture, leaders can create a positive and supportive environment that sets the stage for success in Marine Corps Recruiting.

Lastly, as much as we want every recruiter to succeed, some just don't want to. You need to protect your culture at all costs, and those who are counterproductive need to go. For those cases, it is best to get them off of the duty. You may be down a recruiter and think to yourself, "What would happen if the recruiter leaves, and we are down a sector" to which I would reply, "What would happen if we don't relieve him, and he stays?'.

Tempo

Anecdote – My Parent's Car

Growing up, I remember my parents always bickering about the air conditioning (AC) in our good car (the bad car didn't have AC).

Whenever they were driving together and it was hot outside, my mom would crank the AC all the way up until it was freezing inside the car. She would then turn the heat all the way up until it was blazing hot, much to my Dad's frustration. He just wanted her to set the temperature to a comfortable level, somewhere in the middle, so that she wouldn't be too hot or too cold. But my mom never seemed to listen, and the cycle of adjusting the temperature would repeat itself over and over again. It always led to some sort of argument between them.

Reflection

You may be wondering what that very short story has to do with recruiting but bear with me. Many offices are like my mom in this sense. They get a new mission letter and take it easy until mission day is right around the corner. Then they crank up the heat just to get across the line! It can get uncomfortable because you are working so hard. Then you make mission by the skin of your teeth and you cool off, but you cool off so much that you start to freeze. Before you know it, you need to crank the heat up again! The cycle repeats itself month after month. Jeremy Shorten had a dream for us in San Francisco. He dreamed that we would stop with this pattern of working hard for a short period and then taking it easy for a while.

The solution to breaking the cycle of working hard for a short period and then taking it easy for a while is simple, but not easy. You have to accept the fact that there are no breaks in recruiting. The phrase "make mission, go fishing" is a lie. It's a fake. It doesn't exist. Recruiting is something that needs to be constant. If you aren't constantly filling your bucket, you're going to fail. I have fallen on my face more times than I can count, and it was always because I thought we had the mission in the bag.

There is a bright side, however. Just because you must keep working doesn't mean it has to be miserable. Set a goal for yourself and your team. The goal I recommend is simple: a four-day workweek. Make a pact as a team that you will work your hardest Monday through Thursday, so that you have a three-day weekend every week. This will only work if you and the team commit to it. It's a great goal to work towards, and I'm confident that your team will be motivated to work hard toward it.

Communication

Anecdote – Operation Inherent Resolve, Second Trip

I was deployed to Operation Inherent Resolve in 2021, and it was there that I had the pleasure of serving under Colonel Jeffrey Buffa. A seasoned leader who originally enlisted in the Marine Corps in 1988, Colonel Buffa was an officer that you were truly grateful to have. One of the things that stood out to me the most about him was his commitment to communication. He understood that effective communication was essential to the success of any team, and he made it a priority to keep his subordinates informed and in the loop.

To facilitate this, Colonel Buffa held regular sync meetings, one in the morning and one in the evening. These meetings encouraged vertical and horizontal communication. They also served as an opportunity for his subordinates to brief him on their updates as well as what they needed, and he always listened attentively. He never belittled anyone or tried to play gotcha, and he was appreciative of the work and information being presented.

After his subordinates had a chance to speak, Colonel Buffa would be the last to speak and would end the meetings by "pontificating" (as he called it) about updates across the area of operations (AOR). As a result, people left the meetings informed about all aspects of the battle space and with clear guidance from leadership. The meetings rarely lasted longer than 45 minutes, and Colonel Buffa always tried to end them early, saying something like, "I give you X minutes back of your lives." These meetings were actually valuable, a stark contrast to many meetings enlisted men are forced to endure, and I found myself looking forward to them because of Colonel Buffa's leadership style.

One of the things that Colonel Buffa stressed to me was the importance of teamwork. He believed that if people weren't talking, they weren't a team, and he made it a point to foster an environment where open and honest communication was encouraged. His leadership style was one of humility and respect, and he always tried to listen to his subordinates and take their concerns into consideration.

Serving under Colonel Jeffrey Buffa was a truly enriching experience. He was a leader who understood the importance of communication and teamwork, and he made it a priority to foster a positive and productive working environment. I am grateful to have had the opportunity to serve under him and learn from his leadership.

Reflection

As a Recruiting Sub-Station, it is important to constantly strive for ways to improve and enhance the effectiveness of your team. One effective way to do this is by holding regular morning meetings and evening debriefs in your recruiting office. These regular check-ins can provide a wealth of benefits and help to ensure the success and effectiveness of your team. They create a healthy battle rhythm for your office and give your recruiters a reason to show up in the morning. It is important though that they are conducted correctly.

For starters, use morning meetings and evening debriefs to keep everyone informed and on track. By doing so, you can guarantee that everyone knows where the team is at for mission and what is expected of each recruiter individually. By conducting these meetings daily you can avoid misunderstandings and ensure that everyone is on the same page.

Use these meetings to foster a sense of teamwork and collaboration. Encourage open and honest communication to allow for the sharing of ideas to create an environment that promotes collaboration. This will lead to greater success and effectiveness, as everyone will feel comfortable to contribute their unique perspective and expertise to the team.

Make the meetings an opportunity for team members to receive feedback and guidance. The information goes both ways. A common mistake is for these meetings to turn into the SNCOIC directing every action with zero feedback. By allowing team members to brief their superiors and receive guidance in return, you can ensure that everyone is receiving the support and direction they need to succeed. This can be particularly important for newer recruiters, who may be looking for guidance and direction as they navigate their roles and responsibilities.

Stick to a hard and fast time limit, just as Colonel Buffa did in the previous anecdote. Sticking to time limits in meetings is essential for efficient team collaboration. It ensures the meeting stays on track, respects your Marines' time, maintains focus and alertness, and encourages preparation. Time limits help to prioritize important topics, make key decisions, and assign action items, all while improving productivity, decision-making, and preparedness.

Canvassing recruiters should brief the SNCOIC before the SNCOIC speaks, and the SNCOIC should be the last one to speak. The SNCOIC speaks last in a meeting as it sets the tone for the meeting. It encourages participation and active listening from other team members, allows the SNCOIC to evaluate ideas and suggestions before offering their own thoughts, and enables them to make more informed decisions by taking into account the perspectives of the whole team.

Bottom line is that it is important for Marine Corps recruiting offices to hold regular morning meetings and evening debriefs. By implementing these regular check-ins, you can ensure the success and effectiveness of your team. And if you are a part of an RSS that doesn't sit down regularly and discuss the effectiveness of your recruiting efforts, I would ask, are you even a team?

Classic Honor

Anecdote – What is Classic Honor?

Honor is a concept that has been understood and valued in different ways throughout history. In classical and ancient times, honor played a central role in the way people lived their lives. It was divided into two categories: horizontal honor and vertical honor.

Horizontal honor is the mutual respect and recognition that individuals give to each other within an exclusive group. It is based on a code of honor, which outlines the standards and expectations that must be met to be a part of the group. An honor group is a society of individuals who have committed to living by the code of honor. It is a tight-knit and intimate group of people who interact face-to-face and whose opinions matter to each other. A healthy sense of shame is also necessary for horizontal honor to exist. When individuals fail to live up to the group's code, they lose their honor and the respect of their peers. This can lead to exclusion from the group and shame.

Vertical honor is about praising and esteeming those who excel within the group. It is hierarchical and competitive and is earned through demonstrating superior skills or leadership within the group. To earn vertical honor, it is necessary to first have horizontal honor. Without a baseline of mutual respect among peers, vertical honor means very little.

Honor is a multifaceted concept that has different meanings in different contexts. In classical and ancient times, it was based on mutual respect, a code of honor, an exclusive honor group, and a sense of shame. It was essential for maintaining the respect and honor of the group and for being a person of integrity and character. As Marcus Aurelius wrote, "Waste no more time arguing about what a good man should be. Be one."

Reflection

The concept of classic honor can be applied to a Marine recruiting team in several ways. First and foremost, it is important for the team to have a strong sense of horizontal honor. This means that each team member must be committed to living by a code of honor that outlines the standards and expectations for being a part of the team. This code should include things like punctuality, respect for authority, and a willingness to work hard and put the team's needs ahead of one's own. By adhering to this code, team members can earn the mutual respect of their peers and be recognized as honorable individuals.

It is also important for the team to have a strong sense of vertical honor. This means that each team member should strive to excel in their role and contribute to the overall success of the team. This may involve demonstrating leadership skills, taking on additional responsibilities, or simply working harder and more effectively than others. By consistently outperforming their peers, team members can earn praise and esteem from the group and be recognized as leaders.

In addition to horizontal and vertical honor, it is important for the team to have a sense of shame. This means that team members should be willing to admit when they have failed to live up to the group's standards and expectations. By owning up to their mistakes and working to improve, team members can show their commitment to the group and maintain their honor.

The concept of honor can be a powerful motivator for a Marine recruiting team. By striving to live up to the group's code of honor, team members can earn the respect and admiration of their peers and contribute to the overall success of the team. By embodying the values of honor, team members can also set an example for others and be a source of inspiration and guidance.

The Office

Anecdote – The Army Does It Better

Jeremy Shorten, our RI, came by the office to discuss some ideas he had. Jeremy was an experienced and respected Marine, and I knew that his insights would be valuable. So, I listened attentively as he shared his thoughts on how Marine Corps Recruiting Offices could be run more effectively.

One of the biggest hits to my ego came when Jeremy pointed out that the Army does something better than the Marine Corps. This was a tough pill to swallow, as I have always been proud to be a Marine and I have a deep respect for the Corps. But Jeremy's words hit home because, unfortunately, they were true.

He told me that the Army's office branding is always on point. If you walk into an Army Recruiting office, no matter what, the recruiters are in uniform, and the office is in great shape. The branding is consistent and professional, and it really sets them apart from other branches. Everything in their offices pushes recruits to enlist.

Unfortunately, this is not always the case for Marine Corps offices. If you walk into a Marine Recruiting office on any given day, there's a good chance that the Marines are not in uniform and the office itself may not be in the best condition. The paint might be chipped, the furniture worn out, and the overall appearance may not be as polished as it should be.

This was a tough thing for me to hear, as I knew that it was true. I could do a much better job with how we took care of our offices and how we present ourselves. I knew that this was something we needed to work on, and I was determined to find a solution.

Anecdote – How I Met Your Mother

When I was stationed in Japan back in 2011, just about everybody in the barracks was watching How I Met Your Mother. One episode that stuck in my brain was when Barny showed his apartment and how he made it unappealing to women.

If you don't know, Barny from How I Met Your Mother was always a bit of a ladies' man, and he enjoyed nothing more than meeting new women and seeing where things might go. However, there was one problem that always seemed to crop up: women would often end up staying over at his apartment, and Barny wasn't always ready for that.

At first, he tried to be a gentleman and offer them the comfort and hospitality of his home. But he quickly realized that this was not what he wanted. He enjoyed his freedom and independence too much to have someone else around all the time, no matter how attractive or charming they might be.

Barny decided to take matters into his own hands and furnish his apartment in a way that would make it as unappealing as possible for women to stay. He started by getting rid of his cozy, comfortable bed and replacing it with a hard, lumpy futon. He also removed all the throw pillows and blankets, knowing that these were often the sorts of things that women liked to snuggle up with at night.

Next, Barny turned his attention to the living room. He got rid of the plush, comfortable couch and replaced it with a series of hard, uncomfortable chairs. He also removed all the decorations and knick-knacks that might make the apartment feel cozy and inviting.

Barny then tackled the bathroom. He got rid of the soft, fluffy towels and replaced them with rough, scratchy ones. He also removed all the lotions and potions that women might use to pamper themselves, knowing that these were often the sorts of things that made them feel comfortable and at home. He also made an "automatic seat raiser" so the toilet seat would always be left up.

All these changes seemed to do the trick, and Barny was pleased to find that women were no longer staying over at his apartment. They might have been a bit confused by the strange furnishings, but they seemed to get the message that this was not a place they were welcome to stay. And Barny was happy to be able to keep his freedom and continue living the bachelor life.

Reflection

In the first anecdote, we found that everything in an Army Office is consistent and pushes the recruit to want to enlist, in the second Anecdote we saw that everything in Barny's apartment was getting women to want to leave. The thing we can take away from both stories is that we can use our offices to push prospects in the direction we want them to go. Everything in your office should be pushing prospects to want to sign on the dotted line and having a professional-looking office can help tremendously towards this end.

A professional looking office can create a more inviting and welcoming atmosphere. When people walk into a clean, well-organized office, they are more likely to feel comfortable and at ease.

This can be especially important when you are interacting with potential recruits, as it can help to put them at ease and make them feel more comfortable discussing their future plans with you.

Having a good and clean office can improve efficiency and productivity. When an office is cluttered and disorganized, it can be difficult to find what you need and to focus on your work. A clean workspace can make it easier to find what you need and to stay on task.

Finally, it can help to build and maintain the reputation of the Marine Corps. This goes back to staying on brand like we discussed in part one. When people see a well-maintained office, they are more likely to associate the Corps with professionalism and excellence. □

Wearing Your Uniform

Anecdote – A Confession

During my time on the streets, I often heard my colleagues say that they related better to prospects when they were not in uniform. They argued that wearing their uniform could be intimidating or off-putting to some potential recruits, and that they were more effective when they were dressed in civilian clothing.

While I could understand this perspective, I personally do not believe it to be the case anymore. In my opinion, being in uniform is an important part of your job as a recruiter. It demonstrates your professionalism and commitment to the Corps, and it makes it clear to potential recruits what you are about.

I do believe that there may be another reason why some recruiters do not want to wear their uniforms as much as they should. It is not uncommon for Marines to gain weight while on recruiting duty. Less PT, more work, not as much access to gym equipment, all these things lead to some recruiters putting on a few extra pounds, and it can be difficult to fit into their uniforms as a result. It can be embarrassing for these recruiters to admit this to themselves, and they may feel like they have no choice but to avoid wearing their uniforms as much as possible.

I was guilty of not wearing my uniform as much as I should have while on the duty. In fact, I was probably one of the worst offenders. It could be tempting to take a break from the formalities of being in uniform and relax a bit. But looking back on my time on the job, I realized that I probably lost out on a lot of contracts by not wearing my uniform.

There were a few instances when I decided to wear civilian clothing to an appointment, thinking that it might make me more relatable to the prospect. However, in each of these cases, the prospect was harder to sell. I couldn't help but wonder if things might have turned out differently if I had been in my uniform.

As much as I enjoyed the occasional break from wearing my uniform, I eventually concluded that it was an integral part of my job as a recruiter. Wearing my uniform sent a clear message to potential recruits that I was serious about my job and that I took pride in my appearance. It also demonstrated my commitment to the Corps and its values. These were all important factors that helped to build trust and confidence in the Corps and its recruiters.

I learned that being in uniform was about presenting myself in a professional manner and demonstrating my commitment to the Corps. It was about showing respect for the uniform and the values it represented. And it was about doing everything I could to be an effective recruiter and help my office achieve its mission.

Reflection

As a Marine Corps Recruiter, it is of the utmost importance that you always present yourself in a professional manner. One way to do this is by always wearing your uniform. There are several reasons why this is a valuable practice, and in this essay, I will outline three of the most important ones.

Firstly, wearing your uniform all the time demonstrates your commitment to the Corps and its values. As a recruiter, you are representing the Marine Corps to the public, and it is essential that you present yourself in a way that reflects the high standards of the Corps. By wearing your uniform, you are sending a clear message to prospects that you are serious about your job and that you take pride in your appearance. This level of professionalism is crucial in building trust and confidence in the Corps and its recruiters.

Secondly, wearing your uniform all the time makes it easy for potential recruits to identify you as a Marine Corps Recruiter. When you are out in public, there may be many different branches of the military present, and it can be confusing for potential recruits to know which one you represent. By wearing your uniform, you are making it clear from the start that you are a Marine Corps Recruiter and that you are there to talk about the opportunities available in the Corps. This can be especially useful when interacting with potential recruits who may not be familiar with the different branches.

Finally, wearing your uniform all the time helps to create brand identity for the Marine Corps. When people see you in your uniform, they begin to associate your presence with the Corps itself. This is especially important when you are out in public, as it allows people to easily recognize you as a recruiter and approach you with questions. This can be a great way to generate leads and build relationships with potential recruits.

Being in uniform all the time is incredibly valuable for a Marine Corps Recruiter. It makes it easy for potential recruits to identify you, and helps to create brand identity for the Corps. By always wearing your uniform, you are upholding the high standards of the Corps and making it easier for potential recruits to find and interact with you. These are all important factors that can help you be more effective in your role as a recruiter, and they are worth considering as you go about your duties.

Tips and Tricks for Your Team

1. Make the office welcoming and inviting. A warm and

welcoming atmosphere can make a big difference in attracting potential recruits to your office. Consider adding comfortable seating, decorations, and other touches that make the office feel more inviting. Air Fresheners and plants really help make the office smell better.

2. Update the office furniture and decor. Worn-out or outdated furniture and decor can make the office look unappealing and unprofessional. Consider investing in new furniture and decorations that are modern and in good condition. Putting these request sin your mission restatement letter will get them on the command's radar.

3. Ensure that all recruiters are in uniform. As a Marine Corps Recruiter, it is important to always present yourself in a professional manner. Make sure that all recruiters are in uniform, and encourage them to take pride in their appearance. If Marines are overweight, get them into standards, if Marines stink, make them commit to better personal hygiene.

4. Keep the office well-stocked with brochures and other materials. Potential recruits will often have questions about the Marine Corps and what it has to offer. Make sure that the office is well-stocked with brochures, flyers, and other materials that can help to answer these questions. These materials are also regularly used to give out after interviews, if you do not have the most up to date materials, let your command know and document it in the mission restatement letter.

5. Use social media and other marketing tools to promote the

office. In today's digital age, it is important to use social media and other marketing tools to promote your Marine Corps Recruiting Office. Consider creating a Facebook page, Instagram account, or other social media presence that can help to reach potential recruits and share information about the Corps. See more about this Chapter 2 of this book.

6. Buy a new TV for the office. A modern and high-quality TV can be a great addition to your office, and it can be useful for showing videos and presentations to potential recruits. Don't get rid of the old TV, just put it somewhere in the back of the office in a storage closet. That way when you PCS you can put the old TV back.

7. Get your government vehicles professionally detailed. Clean and well-maintained government vehicles can make a great impression on potential recruits and reflect positively on the Corps. You will have to come out of pocket for this but I promise it will pay off.

8. Buy high speed internet for the office that is off the network. Reliable and fast internet can be crucial for recruiting activities and other office tasks. The NIPR network we use at the offices is not conducive to posting content online or conducting other online recruitment methods.

9. Buy a high quality portable speaker for PT sessions. PT is more fun with music and can help to create a sense of camaraderie and connection with your Pool. In addition, music can help to distract them from the effort and discomfort of exercising, which can make

the experience more enjoyable and manageable.

10. Keep the office clean and organized. A cluttered and disorganized office can be off-putting to potential recruits, and it can also be a distraction for recruiters. Make sure to keep the office tidy and well-organized.

11. Sweat Together. I recommend your office workout together once a week, away from the Poolees. Working out together promotes teamwork and camaraderie. When your team works out together, they can bond over a shared goal and experience. This can lead to a stronger sense of team unity and improved morale, which can have a positive impact on their overall performance.

12. Write down a singular goal for your office to work towards. Whether it be a four-day work week, winning Large RSS of the year, or something completely different, having a singular goal to work towards for a team can be extremely beneficial in helping to create a sense of unity and purpose.

13. Create a climate of it being okay to be wrong. Make it okay to not know the answers. It is important to have a climate of humility in a team because it fosters a sense of respect, openness, and collaboration. When team members are humble, they are more willing to listen to others, admit their mistakes, and learn from their experiences. This leads to a more positive and productive team dynamic, as everyone feels valued and able to contribute to the team's goals. Humility also helps to create a sense of trust within the team, as people are more likely to be transparent and honest with one

another. This can lead to stronger relationships and a more cohesive team culture. In short, humility is essential for building a strong and successful team.

14. Don't work on big Holidays like Thanksgiving, Christmas, or New Years. The juice is not worth the squeeze.

6 THE POOL PROGRAM

Chapter Introduction

As a Marine Corps Recruiter, it is essential to lead your pool with strict discipline. Without discipline, your pool may begin to resent you, become complacent, and ultimately fall apart. One of the key ways to establish discipline is through the consistent application of reward and punishment.

According to Sun Tzu, "Discipline is enforced through consistent application of reward and punishment." This means that in order to effectively maintain discipline in your pool, you must consistently reward poolees for good behavior and punish them for bad behavior. This not only helps to establish clear expectations for your poolees, but it also helps to motivate them to continue to behave in a way that aligns with the values and expectations of the Marine Corps.

Another important aspect of discipline is understanding when to apply rewards and punishment. Sun Tzu also states that "If soldiers are punished before they have grown attached to you, they will not prove submissive; and, unless submissive, then will be practically useless. If, when the soldiers have become attached to you, punishments are not enforced, they will still be unless." This suggests that discipline is most effective when it is applied at the right time and in the right way. If punishments are applied too early, poolees may not yet have a sense of loyalty or attachment to the recruiter or the Marine Corps, and may be less likely to respond positively to discipline. On the other hand, if punishments are not applied at all or are applied too late, poolees may become complacent and lose respect for the recruiter and the values of the Marine Corps.

To maintain discipline in your pool, it is important to strike a balance between rewards and punishment. Rewarding poolees for good behavior can help to encourage them to continue to exhibit positive behaviors and can build morale within the pool. On the other hand, punishment should be used sparingly and only in cases of insubordination or serious misconduct. By using discipline in a consistent and fair manner, a recruiter can establish a culture of respect and loyalty within their pool, which is essential for the success of any military unit.

Ultimately, discipline is a crucial aspect of effective leadership in the Marine Corps. By consistently rewarding good behavior and punishing insubordination, a recruiter can maintain a sense of order and control within their pool. This not only helps to establish clear expectations for poolees, but it also helps to build morale, foster loyalty, and ensure the success of the unit. Without discipline, a pool may struggle to achieve its goals and may even fall apart. As a Marine Corps Recruiter, it is essential to lead with discipline to achieve success and set your pool up for success in the Marine Corps.

Controlling the Pool

Anecdote – Sun Tzu and the Warlord's Concubines

Sun Tzu was a highly skilled and revered military strategist who lived in ancient China during the period of the Warring States, approximately 400 BC. At this time, the region was marked by constant conflict and warfare as local warlords vied for power and territory in the aftermath of the collapse of the Chou Empire. Sun Tzu was known for his expertise in military tactics and strategy, and his teachings have been studied and revered by military leaders and strategists for centuries. His most famous work, "The Art of War," is considered a classic treatise on military strategy and is still widely studied and applied today. Sun Tzu's insights and strategies continue to be relevant and influential in the modern world, and he is widely regarded as one of the greatest military strategists in history. One of the most famous stories involving Sun Tzu concerns a challenge he faced while working as a military trainer for a local warlord. According to the tale, the warlord tasked Sun Tzu with training a group of 180 women, including two of the warlord's favorite concubines, to become a well-disciplined and effective fighting force.

Sun Tzu began by dividing the women into two groups and placing one of the concubines in charge of each. He then set out to teach the women a simple drill, making sure they understood the instructions and what was expected of them. However, when Sun Tzu began giving orders and attempting to lead the women through the drill, they burst out in laughter and refused to follow his commands.

Sun Tzu saw this as a failure on the part of the commanders - the two concubines who had been placed in charge - and decided to take drastic action to demonstrate the importance of discipline and obedience. Despite the warlord's pleas, Sun Tzu ordered the two concubines to be beheaded as an example to the rest of the company. From that point on, the women were said to have performed the drill exactly as instructed, without a single sound or moment of disobedience.

This story is often cited as an example of Sun Tzu's unwavering commitment to discipline and order in the military, as well as his willingness to make difficult decisions to achieve his objectives. It also highlights the importance of effective leadership and the role that commanders play in ensuring the success and cohesion of their troops. Sun Tzu's teachings and strategies have had a lasting impact on military strategy and leadership and continue to be studied and applied by military leaders and strategists around the world.

Reflection

The story of Sun Tzu and the concubines is a powerful illustration of the importance of effective leadership and the role it plays in controlling and growing a group of people. In this story, Sun Tzu was faced with the challenge of training a group of women to become a well-disciplined and effective fighting force. Despite his efforts to clearly communicate his instructions and expectations, the women initially refused to follow his commands and broke out in laughter.

Sun Tzu saw this as a failure on the part of the commanders - the two concubines who had been placed in charge - and took drastic action to demonstrate the importance of discipline and obedience. He ordered the two concubines to be beheaded as an example to the rest of the company, and from that point on, the women were said to have performed the drill exactly as instructed, without a single sound or moment of disobedience.

It highlights the importance of clearly communicating expectations and consequences, as well as the need for consistency in enforcing rules and disciplining those who fail to follow them. A leader who can establish and maintain a sense of discipline and order within their group or organization will be better able to achieve their goals and objectives and will be more likely to earn the respect and admiration of their subordinates.

But while discipline and order are certainly important for any group or organization, they are not the only factors that contribute to success. To truly control and grow a group of people, a leader must also be able to earn the trust and respect of his or her subordinates. This means treating them with respect, recognizing and rewarding good behavior, and showing genuine concern for their well-being.

A leader who can do this will be seen as fair, honest, and trustworthy, and will be more likely to earn the loyalty and admiration of his or her subordinates. This, in turn, will lead to a stronger sense of cohesion and commitment within the group and will set the stage for ongoing growth and success.

To effectively lead a pool, it is also important to be able to communicate with and motivate your poolees. This means being able to clearly articulate your vision and goals, and inspiring others to work towards them. A leader who can effectively communicate and motivate his or her team will be able to harness the full potential of the group and drive them toward success.

The story of Sun Tzu and the concubines serves as a powerful reminder of the importance of effective leadership and the role it plays in controlling and growing a group of people. A leader who can earn the respect, trust, and admiration of his or her subordinates through fair and consistent treatment, and who is able to effectively communicate and motivate the team, will be well on the way to achieving victory.

Appropriate Punishment for Poolees

Anecdote – General Yang Su

During the Sui Dynasty of ancient China, General Yang Su was a renowned military leader known for his strict discipline and swift punishment of those who disobeyed his orders. As he prepared his soldiers for battle, Yang Su would seek out and execute any troublemakers or those who had made mistakes, often numbering in the dozens. This harsh approach was intended to instill a sense of fear and determination in his soldiers, ensuring that they would fight hard and give their all in the face of the enemy.

He was not afraid to make difficult decisions, including the execution of those who failed to meet his expectations. This reputation for swift punishment was not just used as a tactic during battle, but also as a means of maintaining order and control within his own ranks. In the face of potential failure, Yang Su's soldiers knew that they had to fight with all their might to avoid being replaced or punished. This approach may have been harsh, but it was also effective, as the soldiers under his command were motivated to succeed in order to avoid the consequences of failure. Despite the controversial nature of his tactics, Yang Su's leadership ultimately contributed to his successes on the battlefield.

General Yang Su's tactics during the Sui Dynasty were controversial and divisive, with many people arguing that his approach was both excessive and inhumane. His reputation for swift execution of those who failed to follow his orders or fell short in combat was well known, and this fear of punishment was said to drive his soldiers to fight harder and more fiercely.

However, these tactics also had their drawbacks. Many people believed that the constant threat of execution created a culture of fear and mistrust within the ranks, causing soldiers to be more concerned with avoiding punishment than with improving their skills or developing new strategies. Yang Su's reliance on brute force and punishment was seen as hindering the development of the soldiers' skills and strategies, leading to a lack of innovation and adaptability on the battlefield. Despite these criticisms, Yang Su's tactics were often successful in overwhelming the enemy, and he remains a controversial figure in military history.

Yang Su's approach to leadership and military strategy was undeniably effective in achieving victory. His decisive actions and strict discipline instilled a sense of fear and respect in his soldiers, motivating them to give their all in the face of the enemy. While his methods may not be considered ethical by modern standards, they were certainly effective in achieving the goal of victory in ancient China.

While Yang Su's leadership style may not be suitable for all situations, it is worth considering how some of his principles could be applied to the realm of Marine Corps Recruiting. The importance of discipline and motivation cannot be denied, and a clear understanding of the consequences of failure can serve as a powerful motivator for poolees who want to serve in the United States Marine Corps. By setting clear goals and expectations, and consistently rewarding and punishing behavior in accordance with those standards, leaders in the recruiting world can foster a culture of excellence and drive their teams toward success.

Reflection

In the example of General Yang Su, simply put, he punished his soldiers for not doing what he asked of them. If we boil down what we ask from our Poolees to one thing, that is doing what we ask of them. We ask them to show up to PT, show up to pool functions, and ship to recruit training in shape. The importance of poolees attending physical training sessions and pool functions cannot be understated. First and foremost, it is a matter of personal responsibility. When a poolee agrees to participate in these sessions, they are making a commitment to themselves and to their future as Marines. By failing to show up, they are not only letting themselves down, but they are also failing to live up to their commitment. This lack of personal responsibility is something that will not be tolerated in the Marine Corps, and it is essential that poolees understand this from the very beginning.

In addition to the importance of personal responsibility, there are also practical considerations. Physical training sessions and pool functions are designed to help poolees get in shape and prepare for the demands of recruit training. If a poolee fails to show up to these sessions, they are missing out on valuable opportunities to improve their physical condition and increase their chances of success at boot camp. This is especially true for those who may be struggling to meet the physical requirements, as regular participation in physical training sessions can make a significant difference in their ability to meet these standards.

There must be consequences for poolees who fail to show up to physical training sessions when they have agreed to do so. This is not just about punishment, but rather it is about setting expectations and creating a culture of accountability. If poolees know that there will be consequences for failing to meet their commitments, they will be more likely to take these commitments seriously and to follow through on their obligations.

If there are no consequences for poolees not showing up to physical training sessions, it can have a ripple effect on the entire pool. When one individual fails to meet their commitment, it not only impacts their own personal development and preparation for recruit training, but it can also affect the dynamic and morale of the group. If one person is consistently absent and there are no consequences, it sends the message to the rest of the group that it is acceptable to not fulfill their responsibilities. This can lead to a culture of non-accountability and a lack of discipline, which are crucial elements in the Marine Corps.

Additionally, the physical training sessions are an opportunity for the poolees to bond and build camaraderie, which is essential for their success as a team at recruit training. If one or more members are consistently absent, it can disrupt the cohesion of the group and make it more difficult for them to work together effectively. Overall, the consequences for poolees not showing up to physical training sessions are necessary to maintain a sense of accountability, discipline, and teamwork within the pool.

The importance of poolees showing up to physical training sessions cannot be overstated. It is a matter of personal responsibility, a practical necessity, and an essential part of creating a culture of accountability and commitment. Those who are unable or unwilling to meet this basic requirement are not ready to become Marines, and it is essential that there are consequences for failing to do so.

Punishments in a Marine Corps Recruiting Pool should be used as a means of maintaining discipline and order within the group. The first punishment that could be given to Poolees who do not follow orders is a verbal warning. This serves as a reminder to the individual of their responsibilities and the expectations that have been set for them. It also allows for an opportunity for the recruiter to discuss any issues or concerns that may be contributing to the individual's lack of compliance.

The second punishment that could be implemented is a counseling session, complete with documentation in the Poolee's Pool Card. This is an opportunity for the recruiter to sit down with the individual and discuss their behavior in more detail. It allows for a more in-depth conversation about the consequences of their actions and the importance of following orders. The documentation in the Pool Card serves as a record of the counseling session and helps to track the individual's progress.

The third punishment that should be used sparingly, but with effectiveness, is discharging the Poolee from the Pool. This should only be implemented in cases of severe or repeated insubordination, as it serves as a strong deterrent for others in the group. It is important to make the discharge public, as it serves as a warning to others that insubordination will not be tolerated.

It is important to remember that there is no room for insubordination in a Marine Corps Recruiting Pool. It can spread like a virus and make it difficult for the recruiter to maintain control. By reacting to insubordination with firm and fair punishments, the recruiter can ensure that the rest of the Pool is aware of the expectations and consequences for failing to follow orders. Poolees are joining the Marine Corps, and they can expect to be treated in a militant manner. By reacting to insubordination in a strong and decisive manner, the recruiter can draw the rest of the Poolees closer to them, building a cohesive and disciplined team.□

Make Showing Up Valuable

Anecdote - General Cao Cao

As a leader, it is essential to find the balance between reward and punishment to effectively motivate and discipline your troops. While reward can be a powerful tool in boosting morale and fostering a sense of competition within the ranks, punishment is also necessary in maintaining order and discipline. This was exemplified by the military tactics of General Cao Cao during the Han dynasty in China.

General Cao Cao, a well-known and highly respected military leader from China, was a firm believer in Sun Tzu's Art of War and put it into practice during his campaigns. During the end of the Han dynasty, Cao Cao frequently invaded enemy territories and often returned with valuable spoils of war, including rare objects and gold. These treasures were distributed among his soldiers as rewards, with those who displayed exceptional strength and effort receiving the most. By doing this, Cao Cao was able to motivate his troops to give their all on the battlefield, leading to numerous victories. However, those who did not show the same level of dedication were left empty-handed. This system of rewards and consequences allowed Cao Cao to maintain discipline and ensure that his soldiers were always ready to fight and win.

Cao Cao's approach to rewarding his soldiers for their efforts was a crucial aspect of his success as a military leader. By consistently recognizing and rewarding those who performed well, he was able to motivate his troops and encourage them to give their all in battle. This approach not only helped to boost morale among his soldiers, but it also served as an effective way to foster a sense of competition and drive within the ranks.

However, it was not just the rewards that Cao Cao gave out that contributed to his success. He also recognized the importance of punishment as a means of maintaining discipline and order within his troops. Cao Cao was known to be strict with those who did not follow orders or who showed insubordination, meeting out punishment as necessary to ensure that his soldiers remained in line.

One of the ways that Cao Cao punished his troops was by withholding rewards from those who did not perform up to his standards. This approach was particularly effective because it not only punished those who failed to meet expectations, but it also served as a reminder to the rest of the troops of the importance of working hard and giving their all in battle.

Cao Cao's approach to discipline and punishment was not only effective in maintaining order within his ranks, but it also played a significant role in his military success. By fostering a culture of hard work and discipline, he was able to ensure that his troops were well-trained, motivated, and ready to take on any challenge that came their way.

Overall, the use of rewards and punishment as a means of motivating and disciplining troops is a key aspect of effective military leadership. By recognizing the hard work and efforts of his soldiers, Cao Cao was able to foster a sense of loyalty and dedication among his troops, which in turn contributed to his military victories. At the same time, his strict approach to discipline ensured that his soldiers remained focused and disciplined, which was crucial in ensuring their success on the battlefield.

Reflection

Rewards are an integral part of any successful military unit, including a Marine Corps Recruiting pool. Ensuring that your poolees are rewarded for their efforts is crucial in breeding motivation and fostering a sense of loyalty and dedication among your team. When rewards are given intentionally and are earned, rather than given out arbitrarily, they can serve as powerful motivators that encourage your troops to go above and beyond in their duties.

One key aspect of effective rewards is that they should be

delivered without bias of rank. It is important to recognize the efforts and contributions of all members of the team, regardless of their position or seniority. This helps to foster a sense of teamwork and unity within the group, and ensures that everyone feels valued and appreciated for their contributions.

At the same time, it is important to remember that rewards should be given smartly and with consideration for your resources. Rewarding everyone equally or arbitrarily will generate no motivation and can even be demotivating, as it fails to recognize the individual efforts and contributions of your troops. Instead, rewards should be given in a way that encourages your troops to behave in a manner that reaps rewards, such as through hard work, dedication, and a commitment to excellence.

Rewarding your Poolees for their efforts is crucial for maintaining motivation and a positive working environment within your pool. When your troops feel recognized and appreciated for their hard work, it can have a powerful impact on their morale and drive to succeed. By consistently rewarding those who go above and beyond, you can foster a sense of loyalty and dedication among your troops, which can lead to increased productivity and overall success.

It is important to not only reward your poolees for their efforts but also to use punishment as a tool to maintain discipline and order within the ranks. As Sun Tzu states, "Discipline is enforced through consistent application of reward and punishment." While rewards can be effective in motivating and encouraging hard work, sometimes it is necessary to use punishment as a means of correcting behavior and maintaining order.

However, it is important to use punishment wisely and consistently. Punishing insubordination or failure to follow orders can serve as a deterrent and ensure that poolees understand the consequences of their actions. However, punishment should not be used arbitrarily or excessively, as this can create a culture of fear and mistrust within the ranks.

The use of both rewards and punishment is important in building the character and discipline of your poolees. By rewarding their hard work and efforts, you can motivate and encourage them to continue giving their all. At the same time, by using punishment wisely and consistently, you can maintain discipline and order within the ranks. By using both rewards and punishment effectively, you can create a cohesive and motivated team that is ready to take on any challenge.

It is important to publicly present awards to poolees, with the entire pool in formation. Some examples of awards could include a certificate with a custom patch for the RSS, a t-shirt for the RSS, a waterproof notebook, or any other militarily-themed item. Possible achievements to reward poolees for could include the most pull-ups at a pool event, the longest plank at a pool event, the fastest mile and a half at a pool event, promotion to Private First Class for referring two people, or the most class talk referrals in a given month. It may be helpful to draw inspiration for awards from the monthly awards ceremonies at the RS all-hands training. Think about how it makes recruiters feel when they get an award in front of the RS and try to provide that same feeling to your poolees.

Soft Selling

Anecdote 1 – Anne with an "E"

Anne had always been responsible with her finances. She worked hard at her job and made sure to save a portion of her earnings every month. She lived frugally and avoided taking on too much debt. However, everything changed when Anne was laid off from her job a couple of years ago. She had been making a good salary of $75,000 per year, but without a steady income, she was forced to rely on her savings to get by.

As the months went on and her savings began to dwindle, Anne found herself turning to her credit cards to make ends meet. It was a decision she would come to regret, as she quickly began to default on her credit card payments. While delinquency rates in the US are generally lower than their historic average, defaulting on credit card debt is becoming an increasingly serious problem. In 2017, credit card default rates hit a six-year high.

Anne's financial struggles didn't end there. After her unemployment benefits ran out, she decided to go back to school in an effort to improve her prospects and get her finances back on track. She enrolled in a graduate program and now works part-time while attending classes. Despite her best efforts, Anne is still struggling to pay off her credit card debt. It's been a tough journey, but Anne remains determined to get her finances under control and provide for her family.

Anecdote 2 – Mark Cuban and Credit Cards

Self-made billionaire Mark Cuban is well known for his no-nonsense approach to business and personal finance. He has made a fortune through hard work, discipline, and smart investment decisions, and he has some strong opinions on how others can follow in his footsteps. One piece of advice that he has consistently emphasized is the importance of avoiding credit cards if you want to build wealth.

In a blog post from 2008, Cuban stated, "Cut up your credit cards. If you use a credit card, you don't want to be rich." He went on to explain that discipline is the key to getting rich and using credit cards can be a major impediment to achieving that goal.

There are several reasons why Cuban believes that credit cards can hold you back on the path to wealth. First and foremost, credit cards can be a source of temptation and overspending. It's easy to swipe a card and make a purchase, but the true cost of that purchase may not become apparent until the bill arrives at the end of the month. Credit card debt can quickly accumulate, and before you know it, you may be paying high-interest rates on balances that you can't afford to pay off. This can create a vicious cycle of debt that can be difficult to break free from.

Another problem with credit cards is that they can create a false sense of wealth. When you use a credit card, you may feel like you have more money than you really do. This can lead to overconsumption and a lack of financial discipline. It's important to remember that the money you charge on a credit card is not actually yours – it's money that you are borrowing and will eventually have to pay back, with interest.

Finally, using credit cards can be a risky financial strategy because you never know when you might lose your source of income. If you lose your job or experience a financial setback, you may find yourself unable to make your credit card payments. This can lead to default and damaged credit, which can make it difficult to get approved for loans or other forms of credit in the future.

Given these risks, it's easy to see why Cuban advises people to cut up their credit cards if they want to build wealth. Instead of relying on credit, he suggests that people focus on saving and investing their money wisely. This may require making some sacrifices in the short term, but the long-term benefits of building a solid financial foundation can be enormous.

Cuban also emphasizes the importance of developing good financial habits early on. He suggests setting financial goals, creating a budget, and avoiding unnecessary expenses. By making smart financial decisions, you can set yourself up for success and lay the foundation for a solid financial future.

Self-made billionaire Mark Cuban has some clear advice for those looking to build wealth: cut up your credit cards and focus on developing discipline and good financial habits. Credit cards can be a tempting but risky way to finance your lifestyle, and they can hold you back on the path to financial success. By saving and investing your money wisely, you can create a solid financial foundation that will serve you well in the long run.

Reflection

"Soft Selling" in recruiting is the act of telling an Applicant to just "try out" the Pool program to see how they like it. Soft selling in practice, is like living off credit cards. In a soft sell, the recruiter is not gaining commitment from the applicant of going to boot camp but instead gaining commitment to join the DEP.

Soft selling can be a tempting recruiting method, but it is almost always a source of trouble. If you are considering using soft selling to get most of your contracts (or even just one), it's important to understand the risks and drawbacks of this approach.

One of the main reasons why you shouldn't live off soft selling is it is basically lying to Ops. Ops bets on every one of those Poolees to fill ship holes, and these ship holes are conveyed to the highest levels of leadership. If you are pushing out those poolees who were soft sold because they don't want to go to recruit training, you will be forced to pull in people from dates farther out. This can make it difficult to get ahead of your contracting goal and can lead to a cycle of debt that is difficult to break free from.

Another problem with soft selling is the risk of over-contracting. Every contract you soft sell is just adding to what you owe the RS the next month, even if they don't know it now, that debt will come due.

In addition to the risks, soft selling can also be emotionally and mentally draining. It can be stressful to constantly worry about whether your poolees are going to back out on you. This stress can take a toll on your mental health and overall well-being.

Finally, Soft selling can be risky because you never know when the RS is going to need you to move up a shipper. If they need your guy but he is a ghost, you may find yourself putting the entire RS at risk of missing shipping.

The bottom line, you usually should not soft sell. If you have to soft sell to get across the line for the mission, make sure you run it by the RI and Commander. If they are aware you are just selling this guy on the DEP, they can make a note of it for the future. I wouldn't advise the Commander or RI to recommend you do this, but sometimes, you got to do what you need to do to get the RS across the line for the CO's mission.□

Chanting and Memorization

Anecdote 1 – Cults

Cults often use chanting and memorization to reinforce their ideology and beliefs within the group. These practices can help create a sense of unity and cohesion among members and can also be used to hypnotize and manipulate group members, making them more susceptible to the influence of the cult leader.

Chanting, in particular, can be a powerful tool for cults. By repeating phrases and slogans repeatedly, group members may become more convinced of the truth of the cult's teachings and more likely to follow its teachings and directives. The rhythmic nature of chanting can also create a sense of unity and solidarity within the group, as all members are participating in the same activity together.

Memorization is another tactic that cults often use to reinforce their ideology and beliefs. By requiring group members to memorize certain phrases or slogans, the cult can ensure that its message is constantly present in the minds of its members. This can make it more difficult for members to question or doubt the cult's teachings, as they have internalized them through repetition and memorization.

However, it's important to note that not all groups that use chanting or memorization are cults and that these practices can have legitimate uses in a variety of contexts. For example, chanting and memorization are often used in religious or spiritual practices and can be a means of achieving a meditative state or connecting with a higher power.

In the context of a cult, however, these practices may be used to control and manipulate group members. Cults often rely on emotional and psychological manipulation to recruit and retain members and chanting and memorization can be used as tools to achieve this end. By creating a sense of unity and solidarity within the group, and by reinforcing the cult's ideology through repetition and memorization, the cult can exert a powerful influence over its members and make it difficult for them to leave.

Overall, chanting and memorization can be effective tools for cults to reinforce their ideology and beliefs, and to manipulate and control group members. While these practices can have legitimate uses in other contexts, it's important to be aware of the potential for abuse when they are used in the context of a cult.

Cults and the Marine Corps may seem like vastly different organizations at first glance, but upon closer examination, there are some similarities in the way they operate and the techniques they use to achieve their goals.

Anecdote 2 – Comparing the Marine Corps to a Cult

I once heard a joke that there were only two branches of the military, the Army and the Navy because the Air Force is more like a business, and the Marine Corps is a cult. One of the primary similarities between cults and the Marine Corps is the use of strict discipline and rigorous training. Both organizations place a strong emphasis on following orders and adhering to a strict code of conduct. In the Marine Corps, this includes the "Code of Conduct," which outlines the values and principles that guide the behavior of Marines. Similarly, cults often have their own set of rules and expectations that members must follow, and may use punishment or other forms of discipline to ensure compliance.

Another similarity between cults and the Marine Corps is the use of slogans, mantras, and other forms of repetition to reinforce their ideology and beliefs. Both organizations rely on repetition and memorization to instill certain values and beliefs in their members. In the Marine Corps, this might include the motto "Semper Fidelis" (always faithful) or the phrase "The Few, The Proud," which are repeated and memorized to instill pride and a sense of belonging in Marines. Cults may use similar tactics, such as repeating slogans or chanting to reinforce their ideology and create a sense of unity within the group.

A third similarity between cults and the Marine Corps is the use of group bonding activities and rituals. Both organizations use activities such as group hikes, endurance challenges, and other physically and mentally challenging activities to build camaraderie and a sense of belonging among members. These activities can help create a strong bond among group members and foster a sense of loyalty to the group.

Despite these similarities, there are also significant differences between cults and the Marine Corps. One major difference is the purpose of the organization. The Marine Corps is a military organization that serves the United States, while cults often have more nefarious goals, such as manipulating and controlling members for financial or personal gain. Additionally, the Marine Corps operates within the bounds of the law, while cults may engage in illegal or unethical activities.

Reflection

Anybody who read those last two anecdotes and has been to

Marine Corps boot camp will draw some glaring similarities. It is no surprise that during recruit training the drill instructors for the recruits to chant their general orders, their rank structure, their leadership traits, their leadership principles, Marine Corps history, etc. They do it because it builds loyalty, discipline, and obedience. Use these same methods in your pool program and you will find your poolees becoming more loyal, disciplined, and obedient.

These are a few ways that Marine Corps recruiters could potentially use chanting and memorization to develop a stronger pool program:

1. Chanting and memorization can be used to teach and reinforce basic military knowledge and skills. Recruiters could use chanting and memorization to help new recruits learn and remember important information, such as the Marine Corps' values and principles, or basic military procedures and protocols.

2. Chanting and memorization can be used to build camaraderie and a sense of belonging among recruits. By participating in group chanting and memorization activities, recruits can develop a stronger bond with one another and feel more connected to the Marine Corps as a whole.

3. Chanting and memorization can be used to develop discipline and focus. By requiring recruits to memorize and chant certain phrases or slogans, recruiters can help recruits develop discipline and focus, which are important qualities for success in the Marine Corps.

The use of chanting and memorization should be balanced with other forms of training and education. While these techniques can be useful in certain situations, they should not be relied upon as the sole method of teaching and reinforcing military knowledge and skills.

While there are some similarities between cults and the Marine Corps in the way they operate and the techniques they use to achieve their goals, there are also significant differences in the purpose and activities of the two organizations. The Marine Corps is a legitimate military organization that serves the United States, while cults often have more sinister goals and may engage in illegal or unethical activities.

The Pool Tips and Tricks

1. Pool Functions are all hands on deck. Every month needs to be treated as an audit.

2. Use an App like Discord or Slack to manage your Poolees. More on this can be found in Chapter 2 of this book.

3. Plan every Pool Function from now until your last month on the duty, now. Have it thought out and make the dates available to your Poolee when they enlist. Give them no excuse to not show up.

4. Be firm, fair, and consistent with how you treat them.

5. Do not be their friends, be their leader.

7 A MESSAGE TO SNCOICS

Say Less

Anecdote – A Cup of Coffee and a White Monster

As I sat at the local Dunkin Donuts, I couldn't help but smile to myself as I took a sip of my black coffee. I had always been a fan of the bold, rich flavor of a good cup of coffee, and I knew that this one would be no exception.

I glanced across the table at my ARI, Carb, who was busy chugging down his white Monster Energy Drink. I had always been a little bit surprised by his choice of beverage, but I knew better than to judge. We all had our own preferences and habits, and I was just happy to have the opportunity to sit down and chat with him about my goals and career aspirations within the Marine Corps.

As we talked, my ARI shared with me a quote that has stayed with me to this day: "When you are trying to lead your RSS, the more you say, the less important your words appear, and the less in control you ultimately become."

I couldn't help but nod in agreement as he spoke. I had always struggled with finding the right balance between speaking up and being too vocal, and this quote really resonated with me. My ARI went on to explain the importance of being selective with my communication and only speaking when I had something truly important or valuable to say. He emphasized that by saying less, my words would carry more weight and make a greater impact on my team.

We also talked about the importance of being aware of my own communication and recognizing when it was better to remain silent. He told me that it was important to be confident and assertive as a leader, but also to be aware of my own limitations and to admit when I didn't have all the answers. By showing humility, I could build trust and respect with my team.

As we wrapped up our conversation and finished our drinks, my ARI looked me in the eye and said, "Remember, when you are trying to lead your RSS, the more you say, the less important your words appear, and the less in control you ultimately become."

Those words have stayed with me ever since, and I have tried to apply them in my day-to-day interactions with my team. By being selective with my communication and being aware of my own communication, I have been able to build stronger, more meaningful relationships with my colleagues.

Reflection

The quote, "When you are trying to lead your RSS, the more you say, the less important your words appear, and the less in control you ultimately become," highlights the importance of choosing your words carefully and using them effectively when leading a team or organization. It suggests that the more you speak, the less weight your words carry and the less control you have over your team or the situation at hand.

One possible interpretation of this quote is that it is better to be selective with your communication and only speak when you have something truly important or valuable to say. By saying less, you allow your words to carry more weight and make a greater impact. This is especially important when leading a team, as your words and actions will set the tone and shape the culture of your organization. If you are constantly speaking and issuing directives, your team may become numb to your message and less likely to follow your lead.

On the other hand, if you are careful and thoughtful with your communication, choosing your words carefully and only speaking when it is necessary, your team will be more likely to listen and pay attention. This can help to establish your credibility and authority as a leader, as your team will see that you have something valuable and meaningful to say. In turn, this can help to increase your influence and control over your team and the direction of your organization.

Another interpretation of this quote is that it is important to be aware of your own limitations and to recognize when it is better to remain silent. As a leader, it is easy to feel pressure to always have the answers and to speak up in every situation. However, this can lead to overconfidence and a tendency to speak without thinking. By being aware of your own limitations and recognizing that it is okay to admit when you don't have all the answers, you can show vulnerability and humility, which can be endearing to your team and help to build trust and respect.

The quote "When you are trying to lead your RSS, the more you say, the less important your words appear, and the less in control you ultimately become" highlights the importance of careful and thoughtful communication when leading a team or organization. It suggests that by being selective with your words and only speaking when you have something important or valuable to say, you can increase your influence and control as a leader. Additionally, the quote emphasizes the importance of being aware of your own limitations and recognizing when it is better to remain silent, as this can show vulnerability and humility, which can help to build trust and respect with your team. Overall, this quote serves as a reminder of the power of words and the importance of using them wisely to effectively lead and influence others.□

Appeal to Self Interest

Anecdote 1 - A Shipping Hole

In January of 2020, a young Marine was appointed to lead their own RSS as a SNCOIC. For the sake of the story, we will call her

Eve. Starting out as a canvassing recruiter, Eve worked her way up to become the SNCOIC of one of the highest-producing recruiting substations in the station. Despite the guidance and support of her former SNCOIC, Eve couldn't shake the feeling that she had achieved this success all on her own. Her pride and self-assurance overtook any sense of gratitude she may have had for her old boss.

However, in March of that same year, Eve's former boss found himself in a difficult situation. He was down a shipper at the end of the month and was at risk of missing the shipping mission. This failure could even result in him being fired from his post. Desperate and with nowhere else to turn, he reached out to Eve and asked for her help in covering the shipping hole. He reminded her of the ways in which he had trained, developed, and guided her throughout her career, and of the friendship, they had shared. He appealed to her compassion and loyalty considering they worked together so just a few weeks prior.

Though Eve did have an extra shipper at her disposal, she was hesitant to lend a hand. Pushing her shipper up to fill the hole for her former boss meant that in May, she would be left with a shipping hole of her own that neither she nor her former boss would be able to fill. In the end, Eve told her former boss that she couldn't help him and he was left to find a solution on his own. Unfortunately, he was unable to fill the hole and was eventually relieved of his duties and transferred to a different office.

Anecdote 2 - A Poaching Problem

In June 2019, tensions rose between two SNCOICs, Rafael and Marcus, when Rafael brought a troubling issue to the attention of the Operations Chief. According to Rafael, Marcus had violated ethical and procedural guidelines by contracting a high school senior from one of Rafael's high schools, a move that Rafael saw as highly inappropriate. The Operations Chief, understanding the gravity of the situation, gave both men the opportunity to speak their minds and present their cases.

Marcus began by acknowledging the mistake he had made and expressing remorse for his actions. However, he argued that it was in the best interests of both the Operations Chief and the Recruiting Station to allow his recruiter to continue working at the contested school for the remainder of the school year. He pointed out that even though he had taken a contract from another recruiter, the Recruiting Station had still secured a contract and his recruiter had developed a strong relationship with the school in question. Marcus acknowledged that Rafael's team would suffer because of this decision, but he maintained that it was the best solution available given the circumstances.

Rafael, on the other hand, reminded the Operations Chief of all the times he had gone above and beyond for the benefit of the team. He cited examples of when he had moved up shippers, given up contracts, and even covered holes for other offices, all in the spirit of teamwork and cooperation. Rafael argued that these sacrifices should not be overlooked and that he should not be treated unfairly for being a dedicated and loyal team player. He also emphasized that stealing contracts from other high schools, regardless of the potential benefits to the Recruiting Station, was simply wrong and should not be condoned.

After both men had spoken, the Operations Chief requested that they take a break for lunch and continue the discussion afterwards. Upon their return, the Operations Chief carefully considered both sides of the argument and ultimately decided to allow Marcus and his team to work the contested school for the remainder of the school year. While this decision may have been a difficult one, the Operations Chief believed it to be the most fair and practical solution given the circumstances.

Reflection

It is common for recruiters to be primarily focused on themselves, as the nature of their job often requires independence and self-motivation. This tendency towards subjectivity can make it difficult for them to be interested in anything beyond their own experiences and goals. This is unsurprising given the emphasis placed on individual responsibility and pride in recruiting duty.

As a SNCOIC, there will often be times when it is necessary to seek assistance or support from colleagues or superiors. In such cases, it is important to consider the most effective approach for making the request. While it may be tempting to appeal to feelings of feelings or emotion, research has shown that people are more likely to act when they see a clear benefit to themselves. Therefore, when making a request for help, it is often more effective to appeal to the self-interest of the person being asked.

To do this, it is important to carefully consider the motivations and goals of the person being asked, and to frame the request in terms of how it will support their own objectives. For example, if you are seeking assistance with a recruiting event, you might emphasize the ways in which their participation will help to strengthen relationships with local schools or increase the number of contracts secured. By focusing on the benefits to the person being asked, you are more likely to gain their support and cooperation.

Recruiting is a game where the bottom line is all that matters. When going into a discussion, take a second to think about what the personal motivation of the deciding authority is. Do their priorities align with your own? If not, craft your argument in a way that appeals to what matters to them. By focusing on the self-interest of the person being asked, you can increase the chances of success and ensure that your request is met with a positive response.

Plan All 36 Months Out

Anecdote – Clausewitz' Year in Sight

Carl von Clausewitz was a brilliant military strategist and thinker, renowned for his ability to think ahead and anticipate potential challenges and opportunities. His philosophy of planning and strategy has had a profound influence on the way military leaders approach their work, and it can be applied to many other fields as well.

One of the key principles of Clausewitz's philosophy was the importance of planning all the way to the end. He believed that to be truly successful, leaders needed to think beyond the present moment and consider the long-term impact of their actions. This required a level of foresight and strategic thinking that was rare in his time, but that he himself possessed in abundance.

One example of Clausewitz's approach to planning can be seen in his role as a Prussian general during the Napoleonic Wars. As the war raged on, Clausewitz was tasked with leading a small group of soldiers on a critical mission behind enemy lines. The mission was considered highly risky, and many of Clausewitz's colleagues believed it to be a suicide mission.

However, Clausewitz was not one to back down from a challenge. He knew that success was far from guaranteed, but he was determined to do everything in his power to increase the chances of success. He spent countless hours planning and strategizing, considering every possible scenario and developing contingency plans for each. He worked tirelessly to anticipate potential challenges and setbacks, and he was constantly seeking ways to increase the chances of success.

Despite the many obstacles and setbacks that he faced, Clausewitz remained focused and determined. He never lost sight of his goal, and he was always thinking ahead to the endgame. He knew that to succeed, he needed to plan for every eventuality and be ready for anything.

His careful planning and strategic thinking paid off. The mission was a resounding success, and Clausewitz's reputation as a brilliant military strategist was solidified. His example has inspired countless leaders since, and his philosophy continues to be relevant and influential to this day. Through his tireless dedication and strategic thinking, Clausewitz proved that planning all the way to the end was a key factor in achieving success. His approach to planning and strategy remains an invaluable lesson for leaders in all fields, and it is a principle that should not be overlooked.

Clausewitz's approach to planning and strategy was not limited to his military career. He believed that these principles could be applied to all aspects of life, and he dedicated much of his time to studying and analyzing the ways in which they could be used to achieve success.

Throughout his career, Clausewitz remained focused and disciplined, always working towards his long-term goals and objectives. He knew that success was not something that could be achieved overnight, and he was willing to put in the hard work and dedication required to achieve it.

In addition to his strategic thinking and planning skills, Clausewitz was also known for his ability to adapt and adjust his approach as needed. He recognized that to succeed, he needed to be flexible and open to new ideas and perspectives. He was never afraid to challenge the status quo and consider new ways of doing things, and this willingness to embrace change was a key factor in his success.

In the end, Clausewitz's legacy lives on as a testament to the importance of planning and strategy in achieving success. His approach to these principles has inspired countless leaders over the years, and it continues to be relevant and influential to this day. Whether you are a military leader, a business executive, or simply someone trying to achieve your goals and dreams, there is much to be learned from Clausewitz's example. By following his approach to planning and strategy, you too can achieve success and make a positive impact in the world.

Reflection

As an RSS SNCOIC, it is imperative to plan for the long-term. While making mission this month is certainly important, it is only one piece of the puzzle. True success as a leader involves thinking beyond the present moment and considering the potential consequences, setbacks, and twists that may come your way. This means taking a proactive approach to planning and strategy, and always working towards your long-term goals and objectives.

One of the key principles of long-term planning is anticipating potential challenges and devising a plan to navigate them. This requires a level of foresight and strategic thinking that can be difficult for many people to cultivate. However, it is a skill that can be developed and refined over time, and it is one of the key characteristics that sets truly talented SNCOICs apart from the rest.

A great example of this principle can be found in the philosophy of Carl von Clausewitz, a Prussian general and military theorist who is considered one of the most influential figures in the history of modern warfare. Clausewitz famously wrote, "There are very few men-and they are the exceptions-who are able to think and feel beyond the present moment."

This quote speaks to the importance of thinking ahead and anticipating potential challenges and opportunities. In the role of an RSS SNCOIC, this means considering the long-term impact of your actions and always working towards your goals. It means thinking about mission 12 months from now, and even considering what you want your average APR to be when you leave the duty.

Of course, this level of planning and strategy is not easy. It requires a great deal of discipline and focus, as well as the ability to think critically and creatively. However, the payoff is well worth the effort. By taking a proactive approach to planning and thinking ahead, you can set yourself up for success and achieve your long-term goals as an RSS SNCOIC.

Long-term planning allows you to be more efficient and effective in your role as an RSS SNCOIC. When you have a clear plan in place, you are better able to allocate your resources and prioritize your tasks. This can help you to make the most of your time and achieve your goals more quickly and efficiently.

Furthermore, long-term planning helps to reduce stress and

uncertainty. When you have a clear plan in place, you are better able to handle unexpected challenges and setbacks. This can help you to maintain a sense of control and focus, even in the face of uncertainty.

It is not a guarantee of success. There will always be unpredictable twists and turns along the way. However, by being proactive and thinking ahead, you can significantly increase your chances of achieving your long-term goals.

As an RSS SNCOIC, it is important to plan for the long-term. This means thinking beyond the present moment and anticipating potential challenges and opportunities. By taking a proactive approach to planning and strategy, you can set yourself up for success and achieve your long-term goals. By following this approach, you can become a truly talented SNCOIC, respected and admired by your team and colleagues.

Make Winning Look Normal

Anecdote – Boasting about Large RSS of the Year

It was a cold fall day in November when the news arrived at the recruiting station about yearly awards. All Recruiters in the station were present for the monthly all-hands training, but this month was special because the annual awards were being distributed. An RSS had been named "Large Station of the Year" for its outstanding performance and achievement of its mission. The station's commanding officer was thrilled by the news and couldn't wait to share it with the rest of the team.

As soon as the announcement was made, the team at the RSS erupted into cheers and celebrations. They had worked hard all year to achieve this recognition, and they were proud of their success. However, not everyone at the recruiting station was happy for them.

Some of the other recruiters were envious of the team's success and resentful of the attention they were receiving. They felt jealous of the accolades and recognition that their colleagues were receiving. As they watched their colleagues revel in their victory, they had a twinge of resentment.

Despite this, the team at the RSS couldn't contain their excitement. They boasted about their achievement to anyone who would listen, sharing the news with their friends, family, and colleagues. They even put up a banner in the office to celebrate their victory.

The commander's face began to change. At first, he had been thrilled by the news of their achievement and had joined in their celebrations. However, as the seconds passed and the team's boasting continued, his enthusiasm began to wane. He could see the resentment on the faces of his other recruiters, and he knew that this behavior was not acceptable.

Unfortunately, this boasting only served to further alienate them from their colleagues. Many of the other recruiters at the station began to look down on them, feeling that they were acting childish and boastful. They couldn't understand why the team the RSS was so eager to flaunt their success and rub it in the faces of their peers.

As the RSS continued to celebrate, the other recruiters at the station were disgusted. They watched as their colleagues hugged and high-fived each other, their faces beaming with pride. The scowls and scoffs on the faces of the other recruiters were palpable, and it was clear that they were not pleased with the team's behavior.

Despite the tension and animosity that their behavior had caused, the RSS seemed oblivious to it all. They were caught up in their own celebrations, completely unaware of the negative impact they were having on their colleagues.

The commander, seeing the tension and animosity that their behavior had caused, decided to act. He knew that he needed to find a way to restore morale and unity within the team. To do so, he began assigning the team the RSS increasingly challenging missions. He believed that they could handle these tougher assignments, and he hoped that by doing so, he could help them to rebuild their relationships with their colleagues.

However, this approach ultimately backfired. The team at the RSS found themselves overwhelmed by the harder missions, and they struggled to keep up. This only served to further strain their relationships with their colleagues, who saw them as struggling to handle the workload. In the end, their reputation was damaged, and it was clear that they had a long way to go before they could regain the respect and admiration of their peers.

Reflection

"Keep the extent of your abilities unknown. The wise man does not allow his knowledge and abilities to be sounded to the bottom, if he desires to be honored at all. He allows you to know them but not to comprehend them. No one must know the extent of his abilities, lest he be disappointed. No one ever has an opportunity of fathoming him entirely. For guesses and doubts about the extent of his talents arouse more veneration than accurate knowledge of them, be they ever so great." -Baltasar Gracian

Baltasar Gracian was a Spanish Jesuit priest, philosopher, and writer who lived in the 17th century. His words of wisdom, contained in his book "The Art of Worldly Wisdom," have inspired and influenced countless individuals over the years, and his insights into human nature and the ways of the world continue to be relevant and applicable today.

In the world of Marine Corps recruiting, Gracian's words are particularly applicable. As an RSS SNCOIC, it is important to keep the extent of your abilities tampered down to your peers and superiors. By doing so, you are able to maintain an air of intrigue, and prevent yourself from having higher missions tacked onto your mission letters.

Allowing the RS to see only a glimpse of your team's knowledge and abilities can be more effective than revealing everything you know. It allows others to form their own opinions and make their own assessments, which can lead to a greater level of respect and admiration. At the same time, it is important to be careful not to overstate or exaggerate your abilities. This can lead to disappointment and a lack of trust, which can be difficult to recover from. Instead, it is better to let others form their own opinions and come to their own conclusions about your abilities.

By keeping the extent of your abilities unknown, you can maintain an air of stery and intrigue, which can be a powerful tool in the world of recruitment. It allows others to form their own opinions and make their own assessments, leading to a greater level of respect and admiration. At the same time, it is important to be careful not to overstate or exaggerate your abilities, as this can lead to disappointment and a lack of trust.

Additionally, it is important to remember that boasting about your abilities and accomplishments can be detrimental to your reputation. This can lead others to resent you and see you as arrogant and disrespectful. Instead, it is important to be humble and gracious in your successes and to let your actions speak for themselves. By maintaining a good reputation and being humble in your achievements, you can gain the respect and admiration of your peers and superiors and be seen as a competent and effective leader in your Recruiting Station. By following the wisdom of Baltasar Gracian, you can become a respected and admired leader in your Recruiting Station.

□

Never Take Over a Successful RSS

Anecdote – Big Corframs to Fill

It was a bright and sunny day in June when Sarah took over as the

SNCOIC of RSS Smallville. She had worked her way up through the ranks, starting as a canvassing recruiter and working her way up to her current position. She was excited to take on this new challenge and was determined to make the most of it.

Unfortunately, no matter how hard she worked, Sarah found that she was unable to outshine the previous SNCOIC's results. She tried her best to find top-quality prospects and meet her mission, but no matter what she did, it seemed that she was always compared to the old boss.

At first, Sarah tried to brush it off. She told herself that it was just a matter of time before she was able to prove herself and stand out on her own. But as the months went on, it became increasingly clear that she was never going to be able to escape the shadow of the old boss. No matter how hard she tried, she just couldn't seem to get out of it.

Sarah began to feel frustrated and defeated. She had always been a go-getter and a hard worker, and it was hard for her to accept that she was never going to be able to achieve the same level of success as the previous SNCOIC. She started to lose confidence in herself and began to doubt her own abilities.

As the months went on, Sarah's morale continued to decline. She found herself feeling more and more disillusioned with her job, and she began to dread going into work each day. She knew that she was never going to be able to live up to the expectations of the previous SNCOIC, and it was a constant source of stress and anxiety for her.

In the end, Sarah's tenure as the SNCOIC of RSS Smallville was a tragic one. Despite her best efforts, she was never able to outshine the previous SNCOIC's results, and it took a heavy toll on her confidence and morale. She left the position feeling defeated and disillusioned, unable to shake the feeling that she had never been able to live up to the expectations of her peers and superiors.

Reflection

“Beware of stepping into a great man’s shoes—you will have to accomplish twice as much to surpass him. Those who follow are taken for imitators. No matter how much they sweat, they will never shed that burden. It is an uncommon skill to find a new path for excellence, a modern route to celebrity. There are many roads to singularity, not all of them well traveled. The newest ones can be arduous, but they are often shortcuts to greatness.”

This quote from Baltasar Gracián is a cautionary tale for those who aspire to greatness in their careers, particularly in the world of Marine Corps Recruiting Duty. When taking on a leadership role, it is natural to feel a sense of pressure to live up to the expectations set by those who came before us. However, Gracián's words remind us that following in the footsteps of a highly successful predecessor can be a double-edged sword.

On the one hand, stepping into the shoes of a "great man" can be a daunting task. The high standards set by those who have achieved great success can be intimidating, and the pressure to live up to those standards can be overwhelming. It is easy to feel as though one is constantly being compared to the previous leader, and that no matter how much we accomplish, we will never truly surpass them.

On the other hand, Gracián's quote also speaks to the importance of finding our own path to success. It is all too easy to fall into the trap of trying to imitate those who have achieved greatness, but this can often lead to feeling like an "imitator" rather than a leader in our own right. The key to truly excelling in our careers is to find our own unique path, and to be willing to take on the "arduous" journey that may be required to achieve it.

In the world of Marine Corps Recruiting Duty, this means finding ways to innovate and improve upon the successes of those who have come before us. It means being willing to take risks and to try new approaches, even if they may be unpopular or untested. Ultimately, it means being willing to shed the burden of being compared to those who came before us, and to forge our own path to greatness.

Taking over a successful Recruiting Station can be a daunting task, especially if the previous SNCOIC was highly skilled and respected. It can be easy to feel overwhelmed and overwhelmed by the pressure to live up to the legacy left behind.

Gracián's words serve as a warning to those who may be tempted to step into the shoes of a great man or woman. He advises that it is a difficult and often thankless task, as one must accomplish twice as much to surpass their predecessor. Those who follow in the footsteps of a successful SNCOIC may be perceived as imitators, never able to shed the burden of comparison.

However, Gracián also offers hope for those who are looking to make their mark as a SNCOIC. He notes that it is an uncommon skill to find a new path for excellence, a modern route to celebrity. There are many roads to singularity, and not all of them are well traveled. The newest ones can be arduous, but they are often shortcuts to greatness. This suggests that those who are willing to take risks and chart their own path may be able to find success and make a name for themselves in the world of recruiting. It is not easy, but the reward of carving out a unique path to excellence can be great.

Time Does Not Equal Contracts

Anecdote – The "Worst Office" in Recruiting Station Denver

When I first took command of the recruiting office in RS Denver, the atmosphere was heavy with defeat. Morale had flatlined; the team hadn't hit their recruiting mission for several months. The recruiters' gazes were listless, their motivation sapped by the relentless pressure and the exhausting work hours that stretched from the early morning darkness to the late evening's last light. My predecessor, a fine Marine and an earnest leader, had fallen into the trap of equating time spent in the office with results. Driven by the weight of expectations from the higher-ups, he ran himself and his recruiters ragged, leaving them physically present but mentally and emotionally spent.

I knew something had to change.

Fast forward to today, the vibe in the office is unrecognizable from those days. We are comfortably ahead, with the DEP and Held numbers padded out a month and a half in advance. Last fiscal year, we closed out our mission shipping 20 recruits over our fair share. It's a turnaround that's got the whole command group buzzing. So, what flipped the script for us? It wasn't some radical innovation or a sudden influx of willing recruits. It was something much simpler and far more profound: we overhauled our work schedule.

From day one, I introduced a rhythm to our lives that respected the individual Marine, not just the mission. I gave back the mornings, setting aside 0800 to 0900 for the Marines to hit the gym. Physical training is the cornerstone of our readiness, and it was time spent energizing bodies and minds. Then, at 1000, we gathered for our morning meeting in the office. This wasn't just a tactical shift; it was a fundamental change in our approach to the work-life balance.

Our new hard stop at 1800 was non-negotiable. Every day, without fail, we'd head home to rest, recover, and reconnect with our lives outside the uniform. The only exceptions were the days we held Pool PT sessions, extending our day to a mere 1830. And weekends? They were ours again. Every Saturday and Sunday, the office was closed, except for the occasional pool function starting at a leisurely 1200 or the Sundays we spent shipping recruits to boot camp. Briefly, our District CO shifted shipping to Mondays, and it was like a breath of fresh air had swept through the ranks. That change alone was a morale booster that I wish could have lasted, but as with many good things, it was fleeting and out of my hands.

When I first presented my plan to revise the working hours, I was met with stiff resistance from the command. The idea of starting later, ending earlier, and claiming back weekends seemed heretical to the ingrained culture of 'more is more.' Some members of the command group were adamant, their skepticism echoing in sharp tones of flat-out refusals. They wanted me to adhere strictly to the conventional schedule, to not fix what was, in their eyes, not broken. Treading the fine line between respect for the chain of command and advocacy for my Marines, I offered a tactful "no" in response. I stood at the precipice of delivering an ultimatum: if they sought a taskmaster to whip the team into long hours with dwindling returns, then they had the wrong Marine leading this office.

It was Major Tyler Folan, my Commanding Officer, who became the unexpected ally in my corner. He saw the fatigue in the ranks and recognized the burnout for what it was—an insidious enemy within. Major Folan had the foresight to understand that well-being and operational success were not mutually exclusive. With a trust that was as humbling as it was empowering, he granted me the latitude to implement the new schedule. His decision wasn't just supportive; it was an act of courage that cut against the grain of established orthodoxy.

The courage Major Folan exhibited at that moment, the willingness to step outside the norm, is the very essence of leadership that should be replicated across every RS CO in the nation. It's a testament to trusting your leaders on the ground, to listening to new ideas, and to valuing the welfare of the Marines as much as the mission. This trust and courage allowed for a transformation that numbers could justify and morale could validate. For that, my appreciation for Major Folan is boundless. His support was not just a lifeline for my second tour—it was the turning point for our entire office.What we discovered was profound. The additional hours of rest did not make us complacent; they made us more focused, more strategic in our efforts. Recruiters came in fresh, their minds sharper, their tactics more innovative. They began to value the quality of their engagements over the quantity, knowing their time was respected and limited. It fostered a culture of efficiency and precision.

Our productivity didn't just rise; it soared. The camaraderie returned, laughter and banter became the soundtrack of our office, and with it came a wave of success. Our Poolees felt the change too. They walked into an office buzzing with positive energy, an office that looked like a team winning at life, not just at work.

This story, our story, isn't just about changing the clock. It's about recognizing that our greatest asset isn't the hours we grind through; it's the well-being of our Marines. It's about understanding that rest isn't the enemy of accomplishment; it's its ally. We proved that a well-rested recruiter is a formidable force multiplier. And the numbers, the morale, the smiles on my Marines' faces? They speak for themselves.

Reflection

In the bustling ecosystem of a Marine Corps recruiting office, the clock often dictates the rhythm of life. The long-established onset of the day at the crack of dawn has been a sacred cow, rarely questioned, as if the early start were as much a part of the Marine ethos as the eagle, globe, and anchor. But what if this tradition is not a source of strength but a silent stranglehold on efficiency and morale? What if the unyielding march from 0800 to 2000 and beyond is a well-intentioned, but ultimately flawed, strategy?

Let's step back for a moment. Imagine a recruiting office not as a battlefield that requires relentless assault, but as a high-performance team akin to a championship sports team. Daniel Coyle, in his exploration of successful cultures, points out that such teams don't just work hard; they work smart. They focus intensely on productive tasks and equally embrace recovery. It's a rhythmic dance of engagement and relaxation, which, when performed correctly, leads to peak performance.

Now, picture a recruiting office that begins its day at 1000. The Marines have had the time to wake up fully, exercise, eat a proper breakfast, and arrive at work in a state of mental and physical readiness. They're not drained from a too-early start, and their morale is high because they're balancing work with personal life, something that's often lost in the relentless 0800-2000 grind. Here's how this shift can foster an environment where excellence is the norm, not the exception.

1. Synchronization with Civilians' Schedules:

Starting at 1000 aligns more closely with the schedule of the community we aim to engage. High school students are in class, parents are settling into their day, and the community's rhythm is picking up. When our recruiters are fresh and the community is accessible, the interaction is more likely to be productive.

2. Peak Performance Hours:

Science tells us that for many, the peak cognitive hours are later in the morning and throughout the afternoon. By shifting the start time to 1000, recruiters operate during these optimal hours, potentially increasing their effectiveness in engaging with prospects and stakeholders.

3. Morale and Retention:

The mental health of our Marines is paramount. Unreasonably long hours contribute to stress, burnout, and domestic strain, which can manifest in tragic ways. By ending the day at 1600 or 1800 instead of 2000, we acknowledge the humanity of our Marines, offering them time to decompress, pursue personal interests, and be with their loved ones. This acknowledgment doesn't weaken our mission; it fortifies it with loyalty and resilience.

4. Quality Over Quantity:

Working smarter, not longer, focuses on quality interactions over the quantity of hours logged. The value brought to each encounter is higher when a recruiter is sharp, rested, and prepared. It's not the number of hours we pour into work that defines our success; it's the impact made during those hours.

5. Efficient Resource Utilization:

Operating with a lean mindset encourages the judicious use of time and resources. Instead of blanketing the area with a presence, strategic, targeted efforts during key hours can lead to more meaningful connections and outcomes.

6. Demonstrating Effective Leadership:

Finally, this shift signals to the entire Marine Corps that leadership understands and values the well-being of its members. It shows a commitment to adapting and optimizing, not just for the sake of mission readiness, but for the health of the force.

In conclusion, long hours and fatigue are not badges of honor; they are relics of an outdated mode of operation. The real courage lies in challenging the status quo, in daring to align work with natural rhythms and societal patterns. It is in the bold reimagining of what a productive, healthy, and successful recruiting office looks like. A shift to starting at 1000 doesn't just benefit the individual Marine; it strengthens the fabric of the entire Corps, enhancing the mission through strategic, intentional, and compassionate leadership. It's time to set the conditions not just for success, but for sustainable excellence.

Effective Management of Recruiters Daily Tasks

Effective management of recruiters' tasks requires focusing on the "three P's": Prospect, Plant Seeds, and Poolee. These three distinct axis represent different, yet equally important, aspects of the recruitment process that must be attended to daily.

The first axis, Prospect, represents the immediate needs of the present and the mission at hand. This includes urgent tasks and the bottom line that must be met.

The second axis, Plant Seeds, represents the future. These are the seeds planted today that will be harvested in the future.

The third axis, Poolee, represents the young men and women who have already enlisted and committed themselves to join the Corps.

It is crucial to maintain a balance among all three axis, as it will bring regularity to the mission and success to the office. It may be tempting to prioritize one axis over the others, but it is important to make a consistent effort towards all three every single day. Remember, small consistent efforts every day will make become huge results. In this chapter, we will delve deeper into each axis and provide specific ideas on how to tackle them daily. These ideas are not exhaustive, but they serve as a good starting point for you and your team to build upon for achieving balance and regularity in the recruitment process.

Prospect

Prospecting is an essential aspect of Marine Corps recruiting. It involves reaching out to potential recruits in a systematic and deliberate manner. When tasking recruiters to prospect, it is easy to simply tell them to hit a certain number, but a successful SNCOIC does more than that. They also focus those numbers in a specific direction and articulate the goal in a way that is easy for the recruiters to understand. By conveying a specific prospecting goal to your recruiters daily, you will find they are more responsive to tasks and more motivated to work.

This approach was learned from the great Jeremy Shorten, who observed how the Navy prospects. Navy recruiters are not just handed a list and told to start dialing, but instead are given specific names of prospects to contact and screen out every day, with the focus on contact rather than appointments.

By combining this approach with mapping software, as discussed in Part One, we can achieve amazing results. For example, using the mapping software, you can look up fifteen prospects whose homes are near each other. Task the recruiter to first text the prospects something like this:

"Good Morning [First Name] [Last Name], my name is [Rank] [Last Name] and I am your Marine Corps Recruiter. I will be dropping off some informational materials about the Marine Corps to your house later today and am free to answer any questions you have about enlistment options in the Marine Corps."

After all the texts have been sent, task the recruiter to drive to the homes and drop off pre-made information packets directly to their home. If the prospect is there, have the recruiter attempt to engage. If the prospect would prefer some time to look over the material, let them know you will call later that evening. Have the recruiter follow up with all fifteen prospects that evening via phone calls and see how many responses you get. The goal is to generate a minimum of 5 PAC Cards and three appointments a day in this manner.

It is essential that while we may glean valuable insights and techniques from the methods employed by other branches of the military, we must remain steadfast in our adherence to the unique principles and practices that define the Marine Corps. To that end, it is imperative that recruiters are held to a standard of securing at least three appointments per day, with a specific emphasis on the principle of "ASS IN CHAIR." This principle stresses the importance of recruiters actively seeking out potential recruits and bringing them into the office on a consistent and regular basis.

To facilitate this process, recruiters must be provided with comprehensive training and guidance on the most efficient and repeatable methods of securing appointments. Furthermore, to maximize the utilization of time, recruiters may consider scheduling all appointments at the same time. This was something I did when I was a canvassing recruiter that worked well. I scheduled all appointments for 1600, understanding that while some prospects may not show up and some my fail the EST. Even if all prospects scheduled for that day show up and pass the EST, it is considered a positive outcome, as having three qualified applicants in your office is never a bad thing.

Plant Seeds

Contacting new prospects daily is a demanding task and relying solely on recruiter-generated contact is not a sustainable strategy. Therefore, setting aside time daily to establish future business by "planting seeds" is crucial. Planting seeds can be a lot of things, this may include utilizing social media, implementing take-one stands or QR code signs linking to the Marines website, sending out letters (as detailed in the chapter titled "Your Own Direct Mail Program"), organizing class talks, contacting CDRs to come work for you, networking with influencers, and even, most importantly, investing in your own physical fitness.

Plant seeds every day and invest in the future of your programs and yourself, rather than operating on recruiter-generated contracts. Over-reliance on recruiter-generated contracts is equivalent to living "paycheck to paycheck".

Pool

Maintaining regular contact with Poolees is of paramount importance. These individuals are the commodity you have and failure to engage with them on a consistent basis may result in their withdrawal from the recruitment process. Any RSS can recover from a bad contracting month, no RSS can survive a bad Pool Program.

Weekly contact cannot be overstated. To ensure that recruiters are making weekly contact with their Poolees, it is advisable to adopt a management approach like that of a Platoon Commander, by dividing Poolees into three separate fireteams.

Fire Team 1 should be contacted by phone on Monday, Fire Team 2 on Tuesday, and Fire Team 3 on Wednesday. These weekly contacts should not be perfunctory "how are you doing" calls, but rather should follow a structured agenda with a set of standard questions being asked. These questions should be recorded and annotated in their pool card. An example of questions to ask are below:

- What is your ship date?
- What is your job program?
- When is the next Pool Function?
- Are you on track to graduate? (if applicable)
- Can you pass an IST?
- Is your home life stable?
- Are you mentally ready for boot camp?
- What did you think of last week's PT?
- What was the best part of your week?
- Anything else you would like to talk about?

Schedule specific times for these calls. As a pro tip, make the Poolees call you. Instruct them to set their alarm for a scheduled time and hold them accountable to reach out to you. It is important to pay attention to small details to ensure the best results.

Take Some Risks

Anecdote – The New RI

Life's all about taking the leap, isn't it? That's the lesson I learned from Master Sergeant Matthew Renkas when he stepped up to the RI seat at Recruiting Station Denver. He took over as the RI after som "unexpected availability" happened in the billet, and the atmosphere was charged with caution and uncertainty. But Renkas, with eyes wide open to the challenge, chose to step into those boots. He came in just as a band-aid fix after the previous RI was relieved, but decided to take over permanently after just one month.

For a seasoned Master Sergeant, with his sights potentially set on the next rank, requesting orders to Denver was a decision that could have easily backfired. It was a significant risk, one that could alter the trajectory of his career. However, Renkas wasn't deterred. Instead, he committed fully to the role, becoming an advocate for the changes I was trying to implement. He became the second person to give me the latitude I needed to turn my office around. He even let me bring out my mentor, Thomas McKenzie (MGySgt Ret.), out to speak to the entire RS at our monthly all hands training.

It helped that Renkas wasn't just about sticking to the tried and tested. He constantly sought out fresh strategies to improve our recruiting efforts. Whether it was integrating new technology to streamline our processes or bringing the team together for a Mess night to boost morale, he believed in the power of innovation and camaraderie. These moves, unconventional as they may have seemed, were his way of steering the ship through rough waters.

Taking the entire RS out for a Mess night when we were behind on mission might have raised some eyebrows. It could have been seen as an unnecessary risk, especially when the pressure was mounting. But Renkas understood something crucial: morale is the heartbeat of success. By investing in the team's spirit, he wasn't just spending time; he was building it.

His willingness to embrace risk and champion new ideas has been a testament to his leadership. Master Sergeant Renkas didn't just fill the gap; he expanded it, creating a space where growth was possible and where risks were calculated with precision and foresight.

Now, as we look at where RS Denver stands, it's clear that the risks he took have paid off. The station's success is a direct reflection of Renkas's courage to defy the status quo and his unwavering belief in our potential. His approach has taught us all a valuable lesson: the greatest risk sometimes lies in not taking one at all.

Reflection

Reflecting on Master Sergeant Renkas's journey and the transformative impact it had on Recruiting Station Denver, it becomes clear that risk-taking is not just important in the recruiting environment—it is absolutely necessary. In a field as dynamic and unpredictable as recruiting, the willingness to step out of the comfort zone can be the difference between stagnation and progress.

Recruiting is an ever-evolving challenge, with targets that shift and a demographic that is always changing. What worked yesterday may not work today, and certainly not tomorrow. The only constant is the need to adapt, and adaptation often requires bold moves. It's about pioneering strategies that may initially seem unorthodox but have the potential to capture the attention and hearts of a new generation.

Risks push us to innovate. They compel us to question the status quo and to ask, "What if?" This curiosity drives progress. It's the fuel behind finding new ways to connect with potential recruits, whether through social media, community engagement, or altering our schedules to improve work-life balance. If we aren't willing to test new waters, we risk being left behind.

Moreover, risk is necessary for growth—not just the growth of numbers or meeting mission objectives, but the personal and professional growth of the recruiters themselves. When we take risks, we learn. We become more resilient and more adept at navigating the uncertainties that are inherent in the recruiting world. This resilience becomes part of the team culture, fostering an environment where recruiters support each other and work collectively towards innovative solutions.

Master Sergeant Renkas's risks also highlighted the importance of leadership trust. When those at the helm endorse calculated risks, they empower their teams. This empowerment is crucial for fostering a sense of ownership and responsibility, which drives recruiters to perform at their best. It demonstrates a belief in the team's capabilities and judgment, which in turn reinforces morale and dedication.

In hindsight, the successes we have achieved at RS Denver can be traced back to the moments we decided to take a leap of faith. Each risk, whether it succeeded or taught us a valuable lesson, has been a step toward creating a more effective, cohesive, and motivated team.

In the end, the need to take risks in recruiting is about embracing change and striving for excellence. It's about being bold enough to try new things and smart enough to learn from them. It's about understanding that to inspire others to embark on the brave path of service, we must first demonstrate courage in our own practices. The art of recruiting, therefore, is not just in the numbers we achieve but in the leaps of faith we are willing to take.

8 AN OPEN LETTER TO RS COMMANDING OFFICERS

Commanding Officers of Recruiting Stations,

As an 8411 enlisted Marine Corps Recruiter, I wanted to share some thoughts and insights that I hope will be helpful to you as you lead your teams. Being a Marine who is not part of the echo chamber of command group members you see daily, I feel I am in a unique position to be honest with you, so here it goes, a few tips I think will make you more likely to have a successful tour.

Keep the Main Thing the Main Thing. It is critical to note that all assistance goes to individuals on mission letters. If a Marine is not on a mission letter, they are there to support those who are. Only three billets in your command have mission letters allocated to them: yourself, the SNCOICs, and the recruiters on the street; everyone else is support. It is your obligation as a Commander to ensure that your team is completely focused on making mission, which includes prioritizing the requirements of the Marines who are directly responsible for bringing in new recruits. As a cautionary note, do not allow any supporting roles to put more work in the hands of those on mission letters, they are there to relieve work, not add it.

Choosing SNCOICs. Probably your biggest responsibility while in command will be selecting SNCOICs and choosing your SNCOICs will make or break your tour. While top-producing recruiters may seem like the logical choice for these positions, they are not necessarily the best fit for the job. It is important to select SNCOICs who are strong leaders, with excellent communication and interpersonal skills, and who are committed to developing the careers of their team members; sometimes that is a guy who is performing only averagely as a canvassing recruiter. The bottom line is, do not make the mistake of trading a great recruiter for a sub-par SNCOIC.

Horizontal Communication. SNCOIC Conferences are incredibly important, but not for the training that occurs. The most valuable thing that comes out of these conferences is the relationships that develop between your SNCOICs. Their relationships with each other are more important than anything discussed, or any training conducted. These relationships are what will ultimately make your RS a team and drive them to success. It is important to nurture relationships between them and foster a sense of camaraderie and teamwork because if they are not teammates, you are not a team.

Push Power Down. It is important to enabling your SNCOICs to do their jobs effectively. Take care of them, and they will take care of the mission. This means providing them with the resources, support, and training they need to succeed, and being responsive to their needs and concerns. If a SNCOIC is asking you for something, it is because they need it, and if you do not provide it to them, you are giving them a reason for why it is they did not make phase line or mission.

Attitudes. Be wary of "loser attitudes" within your team. Negativity, brown-nosing, and sarcasm are warning signs of a toxic person, and it is important to stamp them out and not let them fester. Positive and supportive team culture is essential for success.

Second Chances are an Opportunity. Consider giving Marines a second chance when they do something worthy of an NJP. When you do, they will have something to prove. A Marine who has made a mistake is an opportunity for you to capitalize on. If you give them a second chance, with the right framing, they may move the world to redeem themselves in the form of increased productivity. Don't allow a third or fourth chance though, kindness can quickly be viewed as a weakness.

Make Ops Work. Never let Operations sit on waivers. The recruiters and SNCOICs did a lot of work to put that waiver together, and it is important to push it up the chain of command as quickly as possible. Sitting on waivers is just one more excuse a recruiter or SNCOIC can grab on to and blame for their missing mission. And in a lot of cases, they are right.

Command Visits. Eliminate useless command visits. These can waste valuable time that could be better spent on recruiting activities. An example of a useless command visit is when the Sergeant Major comes by to talk to the SNCOIC for three hours and pontificate about his philosophy on leadership. An example of a useful command visit is for an RI or ARI to come by and spend a day right next to a recruiter, teaching him to recruit better by showing him how to do it. Important note, an evaluation of recruiting ability is not training. If the RI/ARI is not demonstrating the skills in a real world example, I'd recommend they just not come at all.

Utilize ARIs. Push your Assistant Recruiters Instructors out for training in the field. An ARI should be on the road daily training recruiters and helping them develop their skills and knowledge. Not recruiting "theory", actual recruiting. Have ARIs make phone calls, conduct ACs, or conduct DCs with the recruiters. ARIs are some of the most skilled recruiters you have in your command, if they aren't demonstrating their skills in person, what value are they?

Your Job is Not Easy. I want to remind you that you have the most difficult position in the Marine Corps as an RS Commanding Officer. It is essentially 36 one-month deployments. Worse, most of the recruiters in your command don't care whether you make your mission or not. What they do care about is their fellow Marines in the RSS on their left and right spending time with their families. They will not make a single phone call for you, but they will make a thousand for their brothers and sisters who are with them working every day. Furthermore, most SNCOICs don't care if you complete your mission; nevertheless, by fostering connections among the

SNCOICs, they will care about their fellow SNCOICs to their left and right. You will achieve your objective month after month by putting the correct SNCOICs in positions to capitalize upon these facts.

In conclusion, it is worth reiterating that the role of Commander of a Marine Corps Recruiting Station is one of the hardest in the Corps. Your team members are counting on you to provide leadership and support, and to create an environment that enables them to succeed. I hope that these suggestions will be helpful to you as you navigate this challenging but rewarding role.

Very Respectfully,

Jacob G. McClinton

ABOUT THE AUTHOR

Jacob G. McClinton is a respected authority on the intricacies of Marine Corps Recruiting, with firsthand experience that lends unparalleled depth to his writing. His book, lauded as the definitive guide on the subject, is the culmination of years of dedication and success within the challenging arena of military recruitment. McClinton's distinguished tenure began at Recruiting Station San Francisco from 2017 to 2020. His exemplary performance propelled him into the role of SNCOIC for the subsequent 28 months, where he honed his expertise in strategic recruitment practices.

Currently serving a second tour on recruiting duty in Recruiting Station Denver, McClinton leads a formidable team of recruiters, continuously achieving success and setting benchmarks in the recruitment community. His background in military intelligence within the fleet has provided him with a unique perspective on the needs and strategies of the Marine Corps, enriching his approach to recruiting.

Despite his accomplishments and the prestige of being a recruiter, McClinton has made a conscious decision not to pursue a career in recruiting. His driving force for penning this seminal work is a profound commitment to his fellow 8411s—the dedicated Marines on the street. He seeks to empower them with the knowledge and tactics needed to excel in their roles, enabling them to enjoy more precious time with their spouses and children. His book is not only a professional legacy but also a heartfelt contribution to the well-being of his comrades and their families.

APPENDIX A

Recruiter Reading List

Before 3-Month Evaluation:

"How to Win Friends and Influence People" by Dale Carnegie

"Guidebook for Recruiters: Volume I" by United States Marine Corps

"What Every Body is Saying" by Joe Navarro

"The Referral Engine" by John Jantsch

"Spin Selling" by Neil Rackham

Before 6-Month Evaluation:

"The Challenger Sale" by Brent Adamson and Matthew Dixon

"Pimpology" by Pimpin' Ken

"The Art of Closing the Sale" by Brian Tracy

"The Little Red Book of Selling: 12.5 Principles of Sales Greatness" by Jeffrey Gitomer

"Never Split the Difference: Negotiating as If Your Life Depended On It" by Chris Voss

Before 9-Month Evaluation

"Secrets of Closing the Sale" by Zig Ziglar

"Start With Why" by Simon Sinek

"The Art of Seduction" by Robert Greene

"No Easy Day" by Jacob McClinton

"Crucial Conversations" by Kerry Patterson

"High-Profit Prospecting" by Mark Hunter

"New Sales. Simplified." By Mike Weinberg

"The Obstacle is the Way" by Ryan Holiday

"What it Means to Be a Man" by Major General Bill Mullen

APPENDIX B

SNCOIC Reading List

Manager

"The New One Minute Manager" by Ken Blanchard

"The Sales Manager's Guide to Greatness by Kevin Davis

"Sales Management. Simplified." By Mike Weinberg

Tactician

"48 Laws of Power" by Robert Greene

"Guidebook for Recruiters: Volume III" by United States Marine Corps

"The Prince" by Niccolo Machiavelli

Coach

"Coaching Salespeople into Sales Champions" by Keith Rosan

"Coaching for Performance: Growing People, Performance and Purpose" by Sir John Whitmore

"The Five Love Languages: The Secret to Love That Lasts" by Gary Chapman

"Emotional Intelligence: Why It Can Matter More Than IQ" by Daniel Goleman

APPENDIX C

RS Commanding Officer Reading List

"The Obstacle is the Way" by Ryan Holiday

"What it Means to Be a Man" by Major General Bill Mullen

"How to Win Friends and Influence People" by Dale Carnegie

"Guidebook for Recruiters: Volume I" by United States Marine Corps

"Guidebook for Recruiters: Volume III" by United States Marine Corps

"Turn the Ship Around!" by L. David Marquet

"Once an Eagle" by Anton Myrer

"Switch" by Chip Heath and Dan Heath

"Good to Great" by Jim Collins

"Meditations" by Marcus Aurelius

"The Culture Code" by Daniel Coyle

"Leading with the Heart" by Mike Krzyzewski

Printed in Great Britain
by Amazon

54737334R00126